BIFF AMERICA: STEEP, DEEP, AND DYSLEXIC

Jeffrey Bergeron
(AKA Biff America)

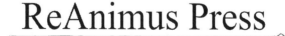

ReAnimus Press
Breathing Life into Great Books

ReAnimus Press
1100 Johnson Road #16-143
Golden, CO 80402
www.ReAnimus.com

ISBN-13: 978-1540808042

First ReAnimus Press print edition: December, 2016

10 9 8 7 6 5 4 3 2 1

To Ellen,
My muscle-legged muse.
Kerouac had Cassady,
Dahmer had Tabasco,
And I have you.

FOREWORD

What this country needs is a good small town newspaper columnist and radio/TV personality with honest compassion, a liberal imagination tending toward kooky, a simultaneously sharp, gentle and hilarious sense of humor that would turn Garrison Keillor green with envy, and a love of people and the environment that comes across as genuine and as soul-uplifting as my dearly departed grandmother's ineffably delicious Toll House cookies.

In my book, Jeffrey Bergeron, aka Biff America, sure does fill that bill.

The columns in this rich collection form one of the more thoughtful and laugh-provoking journeys that I've taken in a long spell. Think of *Lake Wobegon Days* meets *The Little World of Don Camillo.* There's a biting satire aplenty throughout these pages, but it is always couched in a truly humane understanding of our species' tragic-comic fallibility.

Not many writers can bring a tear to my eye in four hundred words or less, but I found myself repeatedly moved, and moved deeply, by these poignant and funny stories.

One minute Jeffrey and his wife are contemplating sexual hijinks in their kitchen sink; next minute Jeffrey is screaming angrily at his good friend, a blind skier dying of cancer, for refusing to sit down for safety on a ski run when ordered to by his sighted guide.

If you don't think it can be real bizarre to almost get arrested for trying to smuggle a pair of quarter-inch nose hair clippers onto an airplane post 9/11, read this book.

Biff America leaves no stone unturned. You will be touched by his trenchant observations on death and politics, and you will probably cringe (and guffaw!) at his story about the guy who escaped almost certain death by biting his own testicles.

There are intriguing dissertations on ski town life-styles, knee surgery and goofy family reunions, pharmaceutics, the worst roommate the author ever had, and the deaths of some of his closest friends.

Some years ago, while Jeffrey was driving his mother to the hospital she would never leave, she saw a bumper sticker — ASK ME ABOUT MY PENIS — and insisted that her son detour from the hospital and follow that car so she could see what the driver looked like.

Many columns start off the wall like that, then end up by breaking your heart and uplifting it at the same time, even when they concern low-flow toilets or trying to buy porn for a friend in prison.

It's an old story: I laughed, I cried, I almost died and I wound up like Yogi Berra, wanting to reread the collection all over again.

This is good stuff, always meaningful, and I promise you:

It will endure.

John Nichols
(author of The Milagro Beanfield War)
Taos, New Mexico
August 2005

CHAPTER 1: RECREATION

My buddy PJ, a world famous jungle doctor, is fond of saying that no one ever looked up from their death bed and said, "Damn, I wish I spent more time working." The love of recreation (and a butt requiring toilet paper) is what separates us from the monkey. I love to ski, bike, hike and camp much more than I like to work.

NORDIC RACING AND BODILY FLUIDS

Backcountry Magazine, January 2004

Phlegm, spit and snot drained from my nose and mouth—my face must have looked like a glazed donut. The searing pain in my buttocks was slightly numbed by oxygen depletion. For the privilege of this profound agony, I paid twelve bucks.

A time trial is a cross-country ski race where participants compete against the clock. This appeals to me because, unlike human competitors, there is the possibility that the clock will break and stop. Racers set out at thirty-second intervals, speeding down a prescribed course. It is not unusual to ski the entire race without passing or getting passed by another competitor. But traveling at my pace, like dripping honey or glaciers, I'm regularly passed by other racers.

I'm not saying that I don't take it seriously. The effort I expend causes me to occasionally leave a lung behind on the snow; my legs often feel as if flesh-eating weasels are nesting in my tights.

Supposedly, many lessons in life are learned from competitive athletics. Part of me feels that sports are simply a vehicle of gratification for the genetically gifted. But I will admit that after more than forty years of competing, I've walked away with a few gems of enlightenment.

One gem goes like this: In life and in races, effort is not always commensurate with pleasure and performance. In other words, sometimes the harder you try, the more you suck.

Before every time trial, I pre-ski the course, timing myself and taking notice of all the hills and turns where I might pull over to vomit. I had skied this ten-kilometer loop hundreds of times, but I decided to do it again slowly a couple of hours before the race. I started my stopwatch and set out.

I picked my way around the slower skiers and lost tourists on snowshoes at a gentle pace. There was no need to hurry so I'd slow down, pass when safe and smile. My relaxed amble allowed me to chat with some people. I joked with some guy skiing in front of a sled containing two screaming children and next to his sour-faced wife. He asked me where the nearest bar was. I saw elk tracks, a ptarmigan and one guy trying to hide behind a sapling to pee. When I finished, I glanced at my clock to learn that the trip took me around thirty-eight minutes with an average speed of about ten miles per hour. The trip was pain free and relaxing, and I had no doubt that I'd do it faster when the time came to push myself.

It used to be when I raced that I'd want to beat some of the fast guys. As I got older, my goal was to beat most of the faster women. It wasn't long before I hoped to finish before my friends' children. And now I aspire to finish before all competitors born between World War II and the Korean War. To reach that lofty goal during this race, I'd have to push myself to great lengths.

Despite being overtaken by two high-school skiers and some guy with a prosthesis (I'm not kidding) during the first couple kilometers, I felt I was having a good race. I moaned in pain for thigh transplants, and with the finish line in sight I sprinted like a man possessed. My clock read thirty-four minutes—that's at a speed just less than eleven miles-per-hour. For all my effort and pain, I had improved by one mile-per-hour.

As I squeegeed the bodily fluids off my face, another lesson sunk in. The difference between a ski where I had time to enjoy myself and smell the flowers, and one that wracked me with pain was a little over ten-percent. To me it didn't seem that the suffering was worth the gain. If we allowed ourselves to enjoy the journey rather than killing ourselves to get ahead, how often would the difference be as negligible? I wonder how many times I've obsessed and worried over a few minutes, a few dollars, while missing the joyful dance taking place all around me.

This story is not an indictment of racing, competition or even the aging process of an ex-jock—I can live with the realities that the years produce and I'll continue to enjoy competition without feeling bad about getting my butt kicked. Instead, it's a reminder to all who care to listen to slow down and enjoy the ride. You might not win the contest but you'll finish with less snot on your face…

~~~

CHUTES, SHOULDERS AND ACCEPTABLE RISK

Backcountry Magazine, November 2004

"Dude, tell me you're doing the chutes and not the shoulder."

Those were the first words I heard when I picked up the phone just after midnight.

"Who's this?" I grumbled.

"Dude, I'm sorry if I woke you, it's Pappy. I'm having a few beers at Fatty's Bar, and Scott said you guys are going up Quandary tomorrow. I was thinking of coming along, but I wanted to know if you're skiing the chutes or the shoulder."

I told him that we probably wouldn't make that decision until we got up to the summit and checked out the snowpack. Because of the recent new snow and high winds, I added that I'd feel a lot more secure skiing the flatter stuff.

Now I like Pappy well enough. But I'd argue that he has more guts than sense, and sometimes I question his judgment.

"Well Bro, here's the thing. That's a long climb. I don't want to make that kind of effort and only ski the flat stuff, so I might join you and ski the south steeps alone if no one else wants to. You hip to that?"

"Sorry Bud," I responded. "If you'd like to come, we'd like to have you join us, but we all ski the same run or at least a run we all agree is safe. I don't want you to jump into something that the rest of us feel is suspect, and leave us responsible for trying to save your hairy butt if something goes wrong."

Pappy wasn't going to give up without a fight.

"Come on Bra, nothing's going to slide. That's a *long* climb to ski a thirty-degree bowl. That's a three-hour climb."

I desperately wanted to say that it was *only* a three-hour climb if, like Pappy, you were hung over, smoked more pot than Bob Marley, and were lugging super-fat skis in alpine boots. What I said instead was, "You know Pap, it seems we're on different missions. Let's each do our own thing and get together on another day."

"That's cool man," he said. "I might see you up there anyway."

I had no doubt Pappy would make the peak that day. He'd get a late start and use the trail we broke to gain the summit. He would then jump into the southern chute alone and be fine. I also knew we'd be long gone before he made his first turn and that we'd need not feel responsible for his safety.

My impatience with Pappy stems from this fact—he makes me feel old and over-cautious. Part of me wishes I wasn't so paranoid when skiing out of bounds. But the other part remembers that old joke: I want to die in my sleep like my grand-dad, not screaming and scared like the passengers on the bus he was driving.

I don't mean to portray Pappy as foolhardy; he's just less cautious than me.

There is a certain element of risk we're each willing to take, and it's generally important to ski with friends whose pucker factor is similar to your own. I've had several friends die in avalanches; twice, I helped locate the bodies. Almost all of them were more skilled and seasoned than me. They were, perhaps, also a little less cautious.

Unlike Pappy, I'd much rather have two hundred turns on a thirty-degree slope, than fifty butt-puckering turns at forty-five degrees. This doesn't make me smarter, or him foolhardy. It only shows the difference in what each of us considers acceptable risk.

This next statement might seem hypercritical coming from someone who makes much of his livelihood working in television, but there isn't a sport or activity that television and video exposure can't screw up. With the glorification of extreme skiing comes a desensitized attitude to the risks. Footage depicting big-mountain skiers on sick lines as slides let loose all around them can entice the rank-and-file backcountry skier to follow suit.

Let's call it the Barbie syndrome. Just like the dolls give little girls unrealistic expectations over the shape of their own bodies, ski films can provide off-piste skiers with a distorted assumption of an acceptable gamble. What most ski movies don't show are the helicopters, rescue personnel and snow-safety experts all working to assure that what looks sick is as safe as possible.

Pappy skied the chutes that day. The snow was indeed stable and the turns were "way-bitchen'-sick Bra." Hearing that, I questioned my own safer, longer, flatter descent from the summit. Then I remembered those people on the bus my grandfather was driving…

~~~

SUMMER SKIING AND MARITAL NEGOTIATIONS

Backcountry Magazine, October 2005

The clock radio displayed four a.m. My wife stood next to the bed staring down at me. In one hand she held a thermometer; in the other was an ice axe.

And she appeared to have zinc oxide smeared all over her face, giving her a cadaverous hue. Waking to those gleaming eyes and the faux-white complexion, I first thought I was attending another sleepover at Michael Jackson's place.

Slowly I regained consciousness and finally realized where I was. "What are you doing with that ice axe, and where do you intend to stick that thermometer?"

Ellen said only, "It's twenty-eight degrees outside…get up."

It's not easy being a summer backcountry skier.

Come June, most of your friends, after suffering through nine months of winter, are ready to move on to warm weather pursuits. This makes it difficult to get partners to come along. And no matter how white the peaks appear from town, unless it freezes the night before, skiing can be both un-safe and un-fun.

When you backcountry ski during summer, skiing is often only a small part of the day. Before actually making a turn, you must wake at four or five a.m. and then drive someplace where you can reach snow. From there you must hike on dirt, on rocks, through willows and over creeks carrying your skis, clothing, food, water, ice axe and crampons in your pack. Once you reach snowline, with any luck it is still frozen enough to hold your weight as you claw your way up to the summit. Finally, you put on your skis and slide.

Usually this fun part occurs about six hours after you've dragged yourself from bed.

Though a ski partner after Memorial Day can be as hard to find as a chess set at the White House, the threat of marital celibacy is often motivation enough to get your husband to join you.

"No slide, no ride." This expression is often bandied about my home—all things considered, it's not too bad of a bargain.

Husbands can be bribed and cajoled, but there is little to be done about the weather.

For the last six weeks, my mate and I had traveled the nation camping in Colorado, Utah, Wyoming, Nevada and California, in search of snow and cold nights. For most of April and May, both weather and snow cooperated. When the ninety-degree temperatures and gas stations posting three bucks a gallon chased us out of California, we returned home to Colorado.

Now before I go any further, I should point out that my mate likes to ski more than anyone I know, which is saying something in a ski town. She spends hours every day looking at maps, reading guidebooks and driving miles just to check out the possibility. It is almost like skiing is her job. (You can leave out the "almost.")

The first ten days back in town she skied nine times. I joined her for most of them. When the weather got warm, well — then she became frantic.

The alarm goes off every morning at four. She checks the thermometer. She curses. Then she'll go on-line and check the temps in the rest of the state. When she is positive that there is no place to ski within driving distance, she climbs back in bed. By then I'm too awake for rest, so I get up and walk the dog.

Optimistic and obsessed, my mate leaves the alarm clock set. After six days of above freezing temperatures, I finally trained myself to sleep through the incessant buzzing and her cursing. Then it turned cold.

Looking at her standing over the bed, I said, "I think I'll not join you this morning, and could you please put down that ice axe...you're scaring me."

Her response: "You've slept in for the last six days, it's cold this morning, you're my only hope. I need to ski."

After a quick process of negotiations, I crawled out of bed and took out the dog, while my mate made coffee.

As my grandfather used to say, "A happy wife is a good investment."

We sat on the top of Mt. Crystal as the sun began to soften up the snow, before pushing off the summit to enjoy two thousand feet of perfect turns on perfect snow. After hiking through mud, dirt and rocks to our vehicle, I was tired and dirty.

As we drove away, my mate said, "I really appreciate you getting up and joining me; I didn't want to go alone. Because you were such a good sport, we can do whatever you want for the rest of the day."

I thought about all my options, and regretfully decided to save my energy. The weather forecast called for a cold night and that meant the next day would be another early morning wake-up call...

~~~

AN OLDER MAN'S INABILITY TO KEEP UP

Backcountry Magazine, February 2002

I'm told that it is a common problem for men my age. And especially for those of us who have married younger women. I wish I could say my young bride was patient with my lack of performance. But rather than gentle encouragement, she screams, "Come on! You can do it. If you can't go any faster you're on your own."

Yes, I'm forced to admit my wife kicks my butt on skis.

Both of us began skiing the same year. While she was only nine years old, I was twenty-one. She took to the sport like I never did. I refuse to blame my inadequacy on our age difference. There are plenty of skiers older than me who also kick my butt. The difference lies in our respective attitudes. I'm afraid of getting hurt. She isn't.

After over thirty years living in ski resort towns, my body is made up of mostly spare parts. I've had three knee surgeries, two shoulder operations and one hair transplant. As long as I've known her, Ellen hasn't even had a head cold. I also have a job to think about — an occupation that many people look at and say, "I could do that," and most of them could. If I got hurt, someone could take my job and do it better for less money. Then I'd be back to loading trucks. Ellen is currently a waitress. If she came to work in a cast, it might only translate into more sympathy tips. But there is little danger of her sustaining an injury since the last time she fell while skiing was back in the late eighties (which coincidentally, was the last time she vacuumed).

I don't mean to make my little love-stallion out to be an insensitive, slope warrior with no consideration for my feelings. She is only that way when she is skiing with her friends — a pack of mean-spirited, man-hating Amazons who love to rub my face in the snow.

I'm not a chauvinist either. My mother was a woman, as well as one of my brothers. But when you get a pack of competitive ladies all vying for a couple of powder lines down a mountain bowl, I've observed the resemblance to a gaggle of gangster rabbits at a salad bar. I've skied with former Olympians who were more inclined to wait for me than the passel of piranhas in pastel-colored soft-shells, whom my wife calls her friends.

Oh, on the surface they're sweet; they are all attractive, many happily married and very polite to my face. But when we get within sight of the mountain, they begin salivating. While putting on their climbing skins, they begin to discuss the day's strategy. This usually involves a heated debate, which some bystanders might label an argument, as each lady makes her pitch for her favorite runs.

Not content to rely on the established names of the surrounding mountains, they have re-christened them to suit their purpose and personalities. "Let's skin up Bad Cramps Peak, ski Compound-Fracture Couloir, then climb back to the summit of Lung Buster. By then we'll be warmed up for some real skiing."

Sometimes a differing opinion will be voiced. "You want to ski Bad Cramps? That is *so flat.* Let's skin up Vertical Drop to Wet Spot Summit, then descend Ball Buster. At least that has a some pitch to it."

After the caffeine wears off and one lady emerges the victor, they explode from the trailhead, leaving me—and the rest of the terrified wildlife—behind. After spitting up a fair portion of my lungs trying to keep them in sight on the climb, I'll reach them on the summit, where they've already de-skinned and are waiting impatiently. With my ski boots still loosened from the skin up, I'm forced to chase after them for the first hundred yards, awkwardly bent over and grabbing at my ankles to get my boots buckled before we hit the steeps of Compound Fracture Couloir.

They usually wait for me midway down the slope (except on big powder days) and occasionally offer tips and encouragement. "You're skiing well, Biff. But if you had cranked down the DIN-setting of your AT bindings your skis wouldn't have come off when you fell off that cliff. You lost several minutes of ski time putting them back on."

After reading what I have just pecked out, I'm afraid I might sound slightly bitter. Well, perhaps I am. It is only natural. I'm a man—a creature known for its large ego. I'm supposed to be the hunter and gatherer in the family. Instead, I'm reduced to frantically chasing after my better half like a Britney Spears groupie. In my own defense, I should point out that there are many sporting pursuits at which I can hold my own, or that I am actually superior to my wife. These include weightlifting, boxing and writing my name in the snow. Sports that rely on strength instead of skill are my forte. Unfortunately, I'm at a time in my life when, for many men, motor skills and stamina begin to fade. Ellen, on the other hand, is just reaching her peak. So, I'm afraid the future holds a lifetime of catch-up for me. But I can deal with that; it is a small price to pay to spend the rest of my life with such a healthy, vibrant woman. A woman whose positive attitude and love of life just might keep me young.

If she doesn't kill me first…

~~~

HEAVENLY JOKES AND A BRUSH WITH A CHURCH BUS

Summit Daily News, July 2002

"He's as shy as a Baptist at an orgy."

As soon as I said those words on television, I wished I hadn't. Not only was it marginally funny at best, it was marginally cruel and, in fact, not true. To the best of my knowledge, I've never encountered a Baptist at an orgy — at least not one wearing a nametag. Normally, I'm not afraid to occasionally venture over the boundary beyond good taste, but lately I've been test-riding a new on-air persona. (I've been hosting a semi-serious news show, attempting to be less ribald and sophomoric, while continuing my practice of butchering the English language.)

My mistake was beginning a sentence not knowing where it would end. When I said, "He's as shy as a…" I had no notion of what was next. That's when "Baptist at an orgy" came to me. Though I felt bad for the Baptists and any orgy participants watching, I did not take the time to have the studio staff edit out those words. The entire process would have taken over an hour and I was anxious to leave. So rather than take the time to be P.C., I took a bicycle ride.

What happened next proves that my God has a sense of humor.

Only an hour later, I was bicycling up a steep, windy mountain road. Traffic was light with only a few cars passing periodically. The air was unusually fresh and the scenery spectacular, yet thoughts of my recent faux pas still lingered in the guilt part of my brain.

Either the vehicle approached silently or my mind was elsewhere, but a big red bus suddenly flew past, missing me by mere inches. I was forced off the road onto a soft shoulder, barely managing to stay upright. I risked a quick look over to see if I was clear of danger and saw this lettering: Praise the Lord Baptist Church (I've changed the name.)

I'm here to tell you the good folks from Praise the Lord got their wish. As the bus nearly brushed my elbow, I had screamed, "Oh my God!"

Once the bus safely passed and I was able to regain the pavement, I waved both hands skyward in a gesture of anger and supplication. Angry that a poor pilot nearly killed me, and a supplicant to God and karma to keep me safe until I got home.

As my pulse rate returned to below four hundred, my mind cleared enough to realize the operator was not malevolent but only trying to steer clear of oncoming traffic. For some reason, I felt that it was better to almost die at the hands of someone careless than someone with malicious intent. And I wanted to speak to that someone operating the bus.

Praise the Lord Church was just up the road a mile.

My exchange with the driver was cordial as I explained that the last time I came that close to death was when I ordered tofu at a NRA rally. He said he remembered passing me, but thought he had given me enough room while still avoiding the oncoming traffic. I suggested that with the roads so thin and his bus so wide, perhaps next time he could wait a few seconds and pass when there was room for all. He agreed, patted me on the shoulder and said, "I'm sorry, brother. Be safe."

As I left the churchyard, I considered the irony. I wondered if God was reminding me that my words, like his wide vehicle, should be used with caution and prudence because they inflict their own type of suffering. Had I taken the time to edit my offending comment, would I have missed my brush with injury? Or might I have encountered another driver with worse results? I'll never know. The one undeniable thing is that roads, like the planet itself, must be shared with consideration and forethought. Intended or not, insults and injuries hurt, whether inflicted by a thoughtless comedian or a Baptist in a big bus...

~~~

BETTER LIVING BY SURGERY AND CHEMISTRY

Backcountry Magazine, March 2004

This story is dedicated to Dr. Janes and Perrinjaquet, the staff at High Country Health Care and Summit Orthopedics.

Local or general anesthesias were my choices. General anesthesia knocks you out like tree skiing without a helmet; local anesthesia numbs you from the waist down. My first inclination was to take the general, but the below-the-belt-numbing intrigued me. With that choice, I would not only experience the operation first hand, but I would be able to fully appreciate how it felt to be a debutante.

In slightly under thirty years of ski resort living, I've been repaired more times than my rock skis. I've had three knee operations (one just last week) a couple of shoulder separations, a strangulated hernia, broken ribs and thumbs, and enough stitches to sew a baseball. I've considered buying a cadaver for spare parts.

If I were born in 1853, instead of 1953, most of these injuries would have left me crippled or dead. But to my good fortune, I live in an era where knees can be rebuilt, bones fused and organs repaired all with rehab shorter than the attention span of an MTV fan.

It was late last summer when I noticed a pronounced 'thunking' sound in my right knee.

I was alarmed. My right knee used to be my good knee. That was until I had my left knee totally rebuilt, which made it my best joint and relegated my right knee to second-best status. That said, until the 'thunking' began, I had few problems with my right side. Sure, when I squatted it sounded like gravel in a blender, but that could be said for most of my joints.

Not being one to take my health for granted, I decided to ask my buddy, the local family doctor, if the 'thunking' was something I should concern myself with. I went to PJ's house and squatted for him. He listened, and then put on his best doctor face and said, "That thunking concerns me. You should see a specialist."

Of course, you know the rest. The specialist strongly recommended I get the 'thunk' removed surgically. He allayed my fears by saying that this procedure was much less involved than my previous total knee rebuild, when he had replaced my ligaments and cartilage with those taken from a lowland gorilla.

If this 'thunk' removal took place as recently as ten years ago, or last week in Arkansas, he would have opened me up like a can of spam. But today, in a state of the art medical facility, the doctor was able to cut three small holes and insert a tiny camera, scalpel and vacuum cleaner into my knee. The camera projected the inside of my joint on a TV monitor in the operating room. By looking at the television while manipulating his instruments, he was able to trim the offending cartilage.

While the surgeon plied his craft with a delicate precision, my job was to lie back, watch the monitor and demand Demerol. Though my doctor-buddy, who originally diagnosed the 'thunk', had assured me that this surgeon was one of the best in the world, I decided that it would be in my best interest to keep an eye on his work; so for a while I did just that. But it didn't take me long to determine he could manage without my help which left me free to enjoy the better living provided by chemistry. My thoughts were, since I'm stuck here for a while and not planning on driving, I might as well cop a morphine buzz.

The next few hours were a blur. I remember being shown a piece of cartilage taken out of my body that looked like a fingernail clipping. A nurse was arguing that I had already consumed enough numbing agents to anesthetize a camel. I also recall my wife suggesting that I assume a more discreet pose in my backless hospital gown. "For God's sake, cover yourself up…you look like you're trolling for a date."

I walked out of the hospital that afternoon under my own power. I was in pain for a couple of days and sore for a few more. A week after the operation I skied, and a few days after that I went back to work (first things first).

I'm almost back to normal—or as normal as I'm capable. And in case you're interested, my bad knee is still the one the doctor just repaired. But as soon as the swelling goes down, he thinks it will then become my good knee. My current good knee (soon to be bad) still feels really good. And most importantly, my wife and I are proud to report that I'm no longer numb from my waist down...

CHAPTER 2: FAMILY

My mother used the 'rhythm method' of birth control and I still can't dance. I'm the youngest of six children in a French Canadian, Boston Irish family. No one ever confused us with the Waltons.

THE FEAR ONLY A PARENT CAN KNOW

Various Colorado Newspapers, *2004*

Only a mother could appreciate how much Grace loved and missed her son, Jimmy.

And Grace knew a fair amount about love and devotion. Only thirty years earlier, before she became a wife and mother, Grace was married to God.

For almost a decade, she served in the Carmelite Order of Sisterhood. In addition to vows of poverty, obedience and celibacy, the Carmelites take the vow of silence. To hear Grace laugh, gossip and sing now, it is difficult to believe that she could have ever remained silent for twenty-three hours of the day.

She didn't leave the convent from any lack of faith or to escape the rigors of the vocation. She took a leave of absence to care for her dying mother.

***

Michael, Jimmy's father, is the kindest, most sincere and generous person I've ever known.

Even as a child he was sensitive beyond his years and gentle. His mother hoped for him to become a priest. Mike loved God and the church, but he wanted children, so he remained in the secular world. Almost anyone who spent time with him could see his goodness. That glow of kindness stood by him through a broken home, a world that was often cruel to gentle people, and the turmoil of the Vietnam War.

The same honesty and compassion that made him special didn't serve him so well during the hedonistic sixties with the opposite sex. It never occurred to Michael to grow his hair, do drugs, and use foul language or to be anything other than the good Catholic boy he was raised to be. Though his mother worried that he wouldn't meet the right girl, I was confident that the right girl would find him.

Grace and Mike met in an Irish pub in Norwood, Massachusetts. She was still on leave from the Carmelites, and enjoying a lunch with her brother. Mike and Grace's brother were acquaintances and he had asked Mike to join them. Introductions were made, and lunch passed easily. When Mike learned his friend's sister was going to be in town for a while, he said maybe they could go to a Red Sox game. Grace heard herself say, "They play the Yankees next week, how about then?" Her brother raised his eyebrows, but said nothing. That doubleheader was Grace's first date in ten years.

Mike and Grace fell in love and married. Their first child was named Jimmy after a Catholic Bishop. Two daughters followed.

I've never met a couple more in love than Mike and Grace. Both are very involved in the Church, their children's lives and the needs of their friends and families.

They raised their children in the same blue-collar neighborhood where Grace grew up. Mike was a loving dad, prone to worry and a little naive. The kids might have gotten away with murder if not for their mother. Grace possessed a worldliness that belied her sheltered past. While Mike was the pushover, Grace would call her kids' bluffs over broken curfews, bad grades or beer on their breath. The children grew up to be normal, happy, sometimes wild, almost always respectful kids.

Mike and Grace took a second mortgage on their home and put all three children through college. Jimmy was the least impressive academically, but like his father he was a late bloomer. In four years, he went from barely getting by to graduating with honors. He joined the Army Reserves to help pay for law school. He worked his way through school, graduated, passed the bar and got a job, while also satisfying his military obligations.

When Jimmy was called up to serve—first in Kosovo, later in Kuwait—he accepted his responsibility with the same good natured resolve that his father did when he was drafted in the sixties. The fact that he was going to be driving a truck, not firing a gun, made his parents feel better on two levels. They didn't want him to be killed or forced to kill another person.

Mike and Grace both had reservations over the morality of war and knew that Jimmy would be safer behind a steering wheel than the sights of a rifle. For over a year, they were afraid to pick up the phone. The daily news of soldiers' deaths made them literally sick with fear.

Their best guess was that Jimmy might be home sometime in February. As the months rolled by, they became more anxious, never dreaming that being even more anxious was possible.

Christmas Eve found Mike and Grace and family at the home of their neighbors. Both families were drinking beer and eggnog before they headed to Midnight

Mass. They drank a toast to friends, family and the Red Sox, and asked God to protect our troops.

The phone rang. The person on the other end asked to speak to either Mike or Grace. Both parents looked at each other in dread, Grace took the call.

The room fell silent as Grace picked up the phone. It was only their priest, asking if they could help with the collection and Communion that night. When she turned back to the room, her son Jimmy was standing in the doorway. "Any beer left?" he said. He'd kept his discharge a secret. They missed Mass that night because Grace could not let go of her son.

So often you hear stories of bad things happening to good people. It's nice to know that is not always the case…

~~~

A FATHER AND SON STORY OF HIGH EXPLOSIVES

Summit Daily News, June 2003

When I was a child in the late fifties and early sixties, the cherry bomb was the Cadillac of fireworks. For those who don't remember, cherry bombs were a powerful firecracker encased in a red container. The explosions they produced were capable of blowing up cans and mailboxes, while producing delight and disfigurement in both children and adults.

Like lawn darts and the Chevy Corvair, cherry bombs were legislated out of existence years ago. I'll grudgingly allow that it was the right thing to do. But when fireworks light the July sky, I know I'll fondly recall cherry bombs, warm Boston summers and a man that many people called crazy — my father.

Fireworks were technically illegal in Massachusetts when I was a child. Usually, the local cops would turn a blind eye to those who had them unless someone complained, property was damaged or someone blew off a finger. And fireworks were not hard to get either. Newsstands and tobacco shops would sell them from under the counter to anyone old enough to have money. But even then, cherry bombs were difficult to find.

My father used to have a long-haul trucker friend pick up a couple of dozen cherry bombs on his way through Florida, so that we'd have some on hand for Independence Day. Even though my brothers and sisters and I would be armed to the teeth with firecrackers, bottle rockets, M-80s, pinwheels and Roman candles, we needed the cherry bombs to blow up the relatives.

A Fourth of July tradition in our family was to light a cherry bomb under the bedroom windows of friends and relatives in the early morning hours. We called it "blowing them up." My father would fill his flask, load the kids in the car and "blow up" six to ten victims on any given holiday. He used to pay special attention to those relatives on my mother's side of the family, whom we didn't much like.

When my five siblings and I reached a certain age, my dad would let us place the bomb and light the fuse. I remember being delighted when I was commissioned to "blow up" my Godmother who always gave me a necktie for Christmas.

My father was considered a bit of an eccentric back then. He was a former boxer and a gambler, he enjoyed a little whisky, and during the depression he managed to come up with enough money to buy a house—no one ever knew how he did it. He was raised poor, ascended to the middle class and once had a drink with Jimmy Hoffa. He wasn't very affectionate to his children, but when my new bicycle was stolen two weeks after Christmas, he went out the next day and bought me a new one.

And he was the only parent I knew who let his kid's "blow up" the relatives. As my brothers and sisters aged, they outgrew the pleasures of the bombings. Every couple of years we would lose another one who thought the prank was immature, queer or some other such adolescent designation that connoted un-coolness. Being the youngest, I participated in the yearly reign of terror well into my teens. The final years found just my father and I carrying on the tradition.

I nearly missed the extravaganza in my twelfth summer due to a ruptured appendix. I was two days out of the hospital and hot with a fever, when my father, much to my mother's dismay, picked me up and placed me in the back seat of the family car. I didn't get to light any fuses that year, but while being carried back to my bed by my father who smelled of gun powder and whisky, I felt like the luckiest boy in the world.

In the terms of today's morals, placing explosives, kids and Jim Beam in the car was irresponsible. Back then, it made me the envy of all my friends. The world was a less responsible, more fun place then.

Between then and now, we've outlawed cherry bombs, made driving while drinking a serious crime and mandated seatbelt and child restraint use. Any parent who broke those laws today, especially enroute to commit an unlawful discharge of explosives, would be considered a bad parent. I'm glad I was a kid when parents were held to lower standards.

My old man died just short of ninety. The year before he passed away, I happened to come home on the Fourth of July. As I remember, the holiday was uneventful. The two of us sat in the sun, missed my mother and watched the Red Sox on television. It was a calm day for a guy with a history like my dad's. But that's the beauty of growing old. You sit back and take pleasure in the woman you loved, the bets you won and the people you've blown up...

~~~

THE SOUND SLEEP OF THE AGED

Summit Daily News, August 2000

Like many of my generation, I have parents who both passed away. Having watched them journey from vibrant to infirm states of being, when I try to visualize them now I never know which era of their life will surface. But the one moment I most often recall was in their later years when I watched them sleep.

I was home for one of my obligatory visits; I didn't want to be there. My hometown was marginally fun when I knew of nothing else. After having seen much of the rest of the world, it was the last place I'd choose to spend my vacation. I got out of the taxi and I walked up the driveway.

On a small cement stoop, barely the size of a double bed, my mother and father sat on folding lawn chairs, asleep and holding hands. Although it was August, they wore sweaters and were undisturbed by the passing traffic.

I approached with a twinge of guilt. They obviously fell asleep waiting for me and I was late. I had run into an old high school friend who was a cop at the airport. We sat in his squad car, drank coffee and talked for almost an hour as my parents awaited my visit.

Due to both love and boredom, my folks would begin preparing for my stay days in advance. My mum would fill the cupboards with my favorite foods (at least, the foods I liked when I was twelve years old). And my father would go out and buy a six-pack of Old Milwaukee beer for our tradition of watching the Red Sox lose on TV.

I quietly watched my parents in slumber. Their heads were tilted back, mouths open and my mother was snoring slightly. Their hands rested on my mother's stained apron with a sunflower print. I thought of a Neil Young refrain referring to his childhood home: "Dream, comfort, memory, despair."

They slept contentedly like tired children. Gone was the stress of raising six kids, running a business and the petty quarrels that filled their younger years. Gone were the concerns over mortgage payments, food bills and bad behavior of their youngest child. In place was the simple pleasure of knowing that this home and this person are the future. If there were any regrets mixed in with their sense of satisfaction and pride, it didn't disturb their sleep. At that moment, old age no longer frightened me. I was able to glimpse the symmetry of the life process and actually look forward to a time when the human calendar would put minor concerns in perspective.

My mother's eyes opened behind her thick glasses and caught me staring. At that moment, for just an instant, I caught a glimpse of her beauty as young girl. She smiled, shook my father and said, "Wake up old man, your son is home."

We went inside and my mother gave me a glass of milk and a Hostess cupcake. I apologized for being late and explained how I'd run into my buddy Danny O'Rielly at the airport. My father said, "Oh, he's got a good job now; he's a state cop."

My mother added, "Did he tell you that he left his wife? We see her in church on Sunday with three kids and no father. It is such a shame."

"Young people don't stay together no more. They ain't got the staying power and it's the kids that suffer," my old man went on. "That's why God made divorce a sin. Do you think I'd still be with your mother if divorce wasn't a sin?"

"Well, you old fool," said my mother. "I'm the only woman in Boston saintly enough to put up with your baloney for fifty-five years. If you think you can do any better, have a look. I bet you a nickel you'll be home for supper."

I don't remember the rest of my visit that summer. After all, it was over ten years ago. I imagine, I spent my time eating bad food, playing cards and watching the Red Sox lose. I'm sure we all went to church. And I'm also sure I was faced with the usual questions from my mother regarding my continued unmarried status. My average relationship, up to that point, had the shelf life of most dairy products.

"Why can't you find a nice girl to marry? You're almost forty; if you're not careful you'll grow old alone. You're like the Lord, you want to love them all, but that won't last forever. I pray every Sunday that I'll live to see your wedding day."

My mother didn't live to see my wedding, but my father did. Ellen wore a string of her pearls; I wore one of her opal earrings.

I enjoy being married. We seldom argue and my wife is my best friend. With work, skiing, biking and different schedules, we seem to be too busy to ever fall asleep sitting in chairs while holding hands. But then again, we have our entire life ahead of us...

~~~

THE MEMORIES THAT HAUNT, IN A GOOD WAY

Various Colorado Newspapers, *December 2003*

They are the ghosts of Christmas past. They are the memories we hold from holidays gone by.

If nothing else, the festive season is an emotional time. Whether from the pleasures of awe and bounty or from the scratched scabs of trauma, a heightened sense of recollection exists for most.

I recall the wonder and magic of my earliest Christmas. Riding my new, second-hand bicycle through a Boston snowstorm Christmas morning, I was dressed for church and thanking God for my parents' kindness. The memory is so clear it could have happened last week. It was only a few years later when that Christmas morning found me with a new BB gun in hand, shooting out our neighbor's outdoor ornaments, thanking God for my steady aim. I asked for a .22 rifle that year, but my parents' thought I was too irresponsible. In retrospect, they might have been right.

The childish pleasures of bike riding and air gun vandalism were soon replaced by adult activities of mistletoe mayhem and intoxicated caroling. Though much of my innocence was long gone, the memories remain pure. But one still haunts me.

It was Christmas Eve day. At sixteen years old, I was licensed to drive a car. I was chauffeuring my mother around the city so she could shop. Traffic was bad, tempers short and parking spots few and far between. My mother had been ill and was still a little weak. I would drop her off at the entrance of the store, park and then meet her at the checkout to carry the bags.

The car was full and we were heading home. It had snowed that day, leaving an inch of slush on the roads. As we traveled slowly with the traffic, we passed a man in a wheelchair trying to get across the street. This happened in the early seventies, before the American Disability Act when life was even more difficult for those with special needs. There was no crosswalk or stoplight in sight. Route 123 was a four-lane thorough-fare that runs through the heart of the South Shore of Boston. He was edging out across the highway, stopping traffic in that lane, but getting splashed by the other passing cars.

We watched him for a few seconds before my mother said, "Help him."

"I'll try to park," I said.

"Park right where you are."

"Here, in the middle of the road?" I asked.

"Stop the car and help him."

I got out of the car to a chorus of honking horns. I ran to the man. He was dressed in Army fatigues, his hair was long and braided and his face showed burn scars. "Can I help?" I asked. All he said was "Yes." In fact, that was all he said the entire time.

We slowly made our way across the road blocking traffic while getting splashed. It wasn't as dangerous as it was embarrassing. On one side of the road was my mum sitting in our parked car blocking traffic, and in the middle were this guy and I blocking traffic. Between the three of us, we had commerce backed up as far as one could see.

I finally made it across the road with the guy and was about to sprint back to the car before the cops came. I saw my mother limping towards us. Watching her pick her way across the four lanes, it dawned on me how little, frail and proud she looked; I met her halfway. She barely acknowledged me as she passed, and instead she walked straight to the man in the chair.

I didn't hear what she said, but she put her hand on the man's shoulder and they both smiled. She then pulled a blue scarf out of her jacket pocket and wrapped it around his neck.

By then, traffic was at a near standstill. Many drivers had seen what had occurred. Traffic stopped and the drivers let us walk back to our car. I imagined out of respect for my mother's kindness.

Once we drove away, traffic began to move again. I looked over at my mother; her eyes were watering from the cold. She said nothing.

"That guy was crazy," I said.

My mother shook her head, "I bet he wasn't always that way."

"I wonder where he lives and where he was going?" I asked.

My mother told me that the large building we had just passed was a Veteran's hospital, and that the man lived there. She said he told her he was allowed leave to Christmas shop for the other guys on his ward.

I remember thinking that despite our differences and personal demons, we all had much in common that day. The expression "There but for the grace of God, go I," came to mind.

We drove in silence until I said, "I hope he liked the scarf you gave him."

My mother laughed and said, "I hope he does, too, it was going to be your present."

~~~

THE POWER OF MEDICINAL LOVE, A MOTHERS DAY WISH

Denver Post, February 2003

As a young child, I once came home early from school to find my mother sitting at the kitchen table crying hysterically.

Her eyes were bloodshot and her mascara was smeared. She looked crazy. When I touched her hand, she stared at me with empty eyes as if I was a stranger. My young mind wanted a comic book explanation— was she under some sort of voodoo spell? Brain-washed? Could she be an impostor?

With an abrupt change of moods (a precursor of her behavior for the next ten years), she seemed to snap out of her condition and said sternly to me, "What happened to your new jacket? It's covered with mud."

I was tempted to tell her it wasn't my new jacket, it was my older brother Mark's (two sizes too big) hand-me-down jacket. Instead, I explained that Walter Casey had thrown mud-balls at me as I walked home from school. Her response was typical. "You should have gotten out of the way. Tell him if he does it again, you'll have your brother Mark beat him up. After all, it was his coat."

I didn't want to explain the difficulties of dodging mud-balls or that if I threatened a beating for Walter Casey, he would beat me up for making the threat. Rather than explain childhood realities and schoolyard vengeance, I had bigger questions and concerns.

"Why were you crying, Mum? Are you sad?"

She sat up straight, dabbed her eyes with a paper napkin and yelled, "Am I supposed to be happy when I send my youngest child to school neat and clean and he comes home looking like a garbage collector?"

That was the end of the discussion. She told me to take off my school clothes and to go outside to play. She warned me to keep out of harm's (and mud's) way and to be home before supper.

That was the first time I realized my mum might be emotionally unbalanced. It would not be the last time I saw her cry. In my innocence, I truly believed that if I kept clean, stayed out of trouble and got passing grades on my report card, I could keep her from being sad.

I also vowed to love her the best I could.

I kept a close watch on my mother for signs of sadness. I was frustrated that my good behavior and affection did little to make her happy. I began to doubt the power of love, passing grades and good conduct. One day, she would not get out of bed; the next, she'd attend church wearing a mini skirt, go-go boots and yell suggestions to the priest. The rest of the family made excuses to attend a different service. I didn't have the heart or courage to abandon her. I'd sit in church and pray with the fervor of a snake handler that she'd remain quiet until we left.

In my early teens, my older siblings, who had left for college and never returned, used clinical words and vague terms to describe my mum's condition. Her best friend, Bridgett, gave me the clearest explanation. "Your mother has bad nerves."

I think a lot of mothers had bad nerves back then. For many, their husbands' jobs and their children's successes defined them. When their kids were grown, and their husbands were working and absent, a sense of purposelessness prevailed. Life was hard on women back then and I think for some from that era it still is.

After her children moved away and my father retired, my mother's nerves gradually improved. My elderly father's failing health and the challenges of running a house on a fixed income once again gave her a purpose. She seemed mostly happy, but would still occasionally cry with little provocation.

Ten years ago, as I sat by her hospital bed, I was old enough to know that like her bad nerves, her cancer could not be cured by love. But at that point of my life, I was convinced that while love had limited results in curing the sickness, it empowers the giver and goes a long way in letting the afflicted know they are not alone in their suffering.

To all you mothers, with bad nerves or not: Happy Mother's Day.

~~~

DEATH, HUMOR AND BODY PARTS

Various Colorado Newspapers, *2000*

"Ask me about my penis."

Now that I have everyone's attention...

That first sentence is not a request for anatomical inquests; those words were written on a bumper sticker. In truth, the car was so dirty and the sticker so old that it might have said "Ask me about my: peonies, pianist or penitence." But to my mother's eyes, there was little doubt about what it said.

It was eleven years ago. I was driving my mum to a Boston hospital for outpatient surgery. She had a few spots on her lungs, and the doctor wanted to take a biopsy. I was scheduled to take her home later that day, but she never left the hospital alive.

We were stopped in traffic and I looked over at her and saw her trying to hide a grimace. I knew better than to ask her if she was okay. We Catholics have been taught to allow others to suffer in silence. Like most of the women in my family, my mother was a stoic. Though she downplayed her condition, I would often see her flinch with pain, and her coughs in the morning would give you chills. I accelerated to the next light.

Our silence was broken when my mother said, "Dear God! Will you look at that?" I followed her gaze to a brown, beat up, old car that looked to have endured many Boston winters.

"Jeffrey, get closer to that brown heap."

I pulled up as close as I could while my mother reached into her handbag and switched her eyeglasses.

She began to laugh and said, "Oh, for the love of God, will you look at what that damn fool has written on his bumper."

I must admit, from my vantage point the bumper sticker did look to be an invitation for a manhood query. Due to both the tension and subject matter, we began to laugh hysterically. After a half-hour of silent angst, it felt so good to laugh. The fear and stress seemed to vent out the windows like the smoke from my mother's Kool menthol. I was willing to enjoy the moment and move on, but my mother needed more information.

"Pull up next to that car. I want to get a better look at him."

I was reluctant to do that because of the traffic, but also from fear that my mother would honor the driver's invitation.

"Mum, you're not going to really ask him, are you?"

"No, I'm a lady. I just want to see what the damn fool looks like."

For the next ten minutes, we laughed like children and chased the brown car. We enjoyed wild speculation about the source of the gentleman's pride. The irony was not lost on me. Here is a grown man driving like a nut with a dying woman in his car who wants to chase a man to ask him about his penis.

We never got a good look at him; he got away.

For the remaining twenty minutes it took us to reach the hospital, my mother could not stop laughing. I hypothesized on the source of the man's conceit and his need to advertise. Laughing seemed to lessen the pain, but when she indulged too much I'd see her recoil. It was as if we were the funniest two people on earth. The thought of him lending his car to his wife or mother brought us to tears.

My mother didn't last long in that hospital. Though the care was exemplary, the health care system was cold and machine like. I have much respect for the nurses and front-line caregivers, but the indifference of her doctor was shocking. During those three weeks, I had fantasies of hitting him.

Despite her pain and situation, for the three weeks it took her to make the transition from matriarch to angel, my mother still liked to laugh. I'd look into her morphine-eyes, set in a scared, gaunt face and mention that bumper sticker. Usually, she would at least smile, sometimes chuckle and always mutter, "that damn fool."

I was always able to make my mother laugh. From childhood impressions of Gomer Pyle to mimicking my father's posture when he woke up with a hangover, I could bring my mother to tears with both humor and bad behavior. Humor kept my family sane (barely). Like many dysfunctional households, much of our mirth was born from pain, but that's okay — sometimes the ends justify the means.

I go back to Boston a couple of times every year and always reminisce about that brown car and bumper sticker. If I ever do run into that guy again, this time I won't let him get away. I'll chase him down to say thank you...

~~~

A LESSON IN PIE EATING AND POVERTY

Altitudes Magazine, 1999

He is eighty-eight years old. He lives alone and on a fixed income. His wife of a half-century is five years gone. He spends his time watching television, playing cards and cursing the Red Sox. He was born in 1910 into a family of five boys and one sister during a time when contentment was often judged by the amount of food on the table.

My dad was always a saver. When he was twenty-two years old, he gave his parents one thousand dollars (a phenomenal amount of money in those days) to keep the bank from foreclosing on their home. He had amassed that money during thirteen years of menial jobs. He was considered frugal in an era when frugality was a way of life.

Even after he achieved a degree of financial comfort, he continued on his course of fiscal conservatism. (My mother called him cheap.)

My memory is filled with stories of hardship that illustrated the poverty of his childhood compared to the relative comfort of mine. My siblings and I would cringe when he would regale us with tales of woe regarding family dinners of lard and sugar on stale bread and of cold winters with little coal. We laughed privately at his admonishments to take only two-minute showers and his conservation of toilet paper.

I began working when I was fourteen so I'd not have to argue when I wanted to buy a new leather jacket, switchblade knife or other adolescent necessities. Each new purchase would be met with an observation: "Twenty dollars for a pair of sneakers...when I was a boy, our family had only one pair of shoes for the six of us to share. It was twelve days before I got to wear the left one."

I will say, he was true to his word of not forbidding me to spend my earned cash any way that I chose. He would strongly encourage me to save some. "You might want to put some cash aside for college," he'd caution. "Just in case they don't have one in your prison." (Though cheap, he always had a sense of humor.)

I left home at age eighteen, not for college or prison, but for Colorado. It wasn't until I was truly on my own that I understood the truth in his many budgetary cliques. His overused sayings like, "Take care of your pennies, the dollars will take care of themselves," and, "wasted time and money are never recovered," began to make sense. It was then that one of my worst fears became a reality; I was turning into my father.

Even at age eighty-eight, my father is still good company. I try to make it home several times a year to spend a few days with him. We pass the time playing cribbage, eating generic food and watching television. He has the short-term memory of a marijuana farmer, but still has a vivid recollection of more than eighty years passed. He'll recount the same stories that bored me when I was a teenager. But now I find myself strangely enthralled.

His lifestyle drives doctors crazy. In addition to an occasional sampling of Jack Daniels, he'll eat cold cereal for dinner and pie for breakfast. "What's it gonna do, kill me?" he'll ask. He eats and drinks when and whatever he chooses. We'll be playing cards and in the middle of a hand, he'll look up with eyes that gleam and say, "Let's go get some pie."

There are several bakeries close by, but he travels to the next town to buy his rhubarb pie from a plump woman named Angie. "Never buy pie from a skinny girl," he said. "That would be like taking dance lessons from a gal with a club foot." My old man was born before they invented sensitivity.

"Be careful with that pie, it cost seven dollars," cautioned my dad.

It was about three minutes after he issued his warning that I dropped the pie on our front steps. I was trying to unlock the front door while simultaneously keeping the screen open with my hip. The rhubarb pie lay on the bricks like a bloody heap. It was ruined. I felt sick. I looked at my father and saw him laughing.

"Remind me not to let you be one of my pallbearers."

Ten years ago, he would have been upset. Twenty years ago, he would have been angry. Now, we simply jump back into his car and drove back to Angie's.

It's funny how age helps prioritize what's important. To a man facing his final years on earth, wasted food and money seem of less consequence. Now wasted time? That is another matter…

CHAPTER 3: PEOPLE

I am blessed with only two God given talents – I can fill a roll of quarters using only my left foot and tongue, and I have a good memory for encounters and conversations. Here is a collection of columns about folks I've met on the road of life – many of whom don't remember me at all.

ROADSIDE TEARS

Summit Free Press, June 1999

Life is a crapshoot. You do everything you feel is right and follow the rules, and still chance, karma, bad luck or whatever can rear its ugly head and bite you in the butt. Conversely, good fortune is also often unearned. So many of the positive things in my life — relationships, marriage, jobs, health — happened merely by me being in the right place at the right time.

The same could be said for learning experiences and close encounters with strangers. These chance meetings occur by luck and kismet, just as often as they do by being receptive, available and open to making contact with others.

My belief in this notion was hardened after an experience on a bike ride in one of Utah's National Parks. The day was ending and the low sun reflected off the red walls in the canyons below. Our camper was parked about twenty miles down the road in the National Forest, just outside the park boundary. Ellen was hiking with some friends, so I was on my own. Ten miles past my turn-around point, I was riding a mostly downhill stretch of highway back to the camper when I heard a hiss from my front tire.

Luckily, I was able to stop safely and get to the side of the road. The second good break came as I coasted to a stop beside an incredibly scenic pull-off, complete with a picnic table — the perfect place to change a flat tire. The parking lot was empty except for a dusty passenger car with Indiana plates. I carried my bicycle past the car, brimming with luggage, and toward the viewpoint. Sitting at the picnic table was a middle-aged woman wearing a t-shirt and sweatpants. She looked like someone's mother and she looked like she was crying. I smiled, said hello and sat on a nearby rock in hopes that I'd be able to fix my flat and enjoy the view, while giving her some privacy.

If I could have stopped someplace else, I would have. She looked like she needed to be alone and I felt awkward interrupting her grief. I tried to imagine her situation. Was she mourning a death, going through a separation or crying over an argument? I assumed her pain involved another person. Her car was packed with coolers, toys, maps and clothing, so she couldn't have been traveling alone.

I silently worked on my bike. The setting sun made everything warm with a scarlet tint. Two hawks soared on the thermals, playing in the wind. They were hovering hundreds of feet from the canyon floor, but for the two of us sitting on the rim, they were at eye level.

When I heard her sob, I glanced over at her again.

I observed her to be in her fifties, maybe middle income and of fading beauty. Her hair, once blonde, was now brassy and gray, and her clothing suggested suburbia. I could picture her picking up kids up at soccer practice and cooking up a meal of macaroni and cheese.

She sobbed again.

Her crying was making me very uncomfortable. With my flat fixed, all that remained was to pump the tire up. I decided to do it elsewhere.

I picked up my bike and walked to the side of the road, where I planned to finish the job. My bike shoes crunched on the gravel, which caught her attention. As I headed back to the highway, I heard her say over my shoulder. "I'm sorry to chase you away."

"That's okay," I replied. "I'm done. It's getting dark. I have to get going."

She didn't say anything else.

Before I continued to the road, I stopped to offer, "I'm sorry you're sad."

While I half expected an explanation regarding her condition, she instead simply said, "Today's my birthday. I'm forty-nine years old, and I've lived my entire life for other people. Don't ever do that."

Had I thought about it longer, I could have come up with something more stupid to say then my actual response, but it would have taken me a while. "I won't."

After dinner that night, Ellen and I listened to my shortwave radio. We had picked up the BBC Network, which was broadcasting from London. A very crisp, emotionless British accent announced the reports on various disasters around the globe. He mentioned another bombing in the Middle East, a tragic bus crash in India, atrocities in Bogotá, as well as a schoolyard shooting in America. The news was dire and depressing and starkly contrasted our serene setting.

"Let's shut off that thing," she said. "There is too much sadness around the world, no sense bringing it to a place as beautiful as this."

I turned off the news and looked at the sky. I thought of the lady in the rest area and others saddened in our world. I was reminded again how random life can be. You can play by the rules, work hard, do as you're told, and you can still find yourself crying by the side of the road on your birthday.

Shooting stars filled the sky and the wind rustled leaves in the cottonwoods. I considered what adventure the next day was going to bring. I wondered how the rest-area lady was doing at that moment. I hoped she felt better; I hoped she felt loved and appreciated.

As I, at that moment, did feel loved and appreciated, as well as undeserving and blessed. I can't say I felt guilty, just lucky.

Good fortune is wasted unless recognized…

~~~

CRIMES THAT DON'T PUT YOU IN JAIL

Vail Daily News, 2003

Jerry spent seven years in prison. His sins ranged from racketeering to conspiracy to tax evasion. He was a career criminal.

He is also my best friend's older brother, so we more or less grew up together. Even as a kid, Jerry was wild. With the devil's persuasion, he'd talk my buddy Bobby and me into joining him in petty crimes. We'd get caught, he wouldn't.

Somewhere on the road to adulthood, Bobby and I mended our ways, while Jerry continued to behave badly. A six- to ten-year sentence was the final result.

Jerry had been out only a few weeks when he made the eighteen-hour drive to attend my father's funeral. He appeared muscular, but thin. And despite the long scar over his eyebrow, he still had the same look of that mischievous little boy.

He wasn't the only old friend who went out of his way to be at my old man's service. Six of "my son's hoodlum friends" (as my father used to refer to them), now in various states of health and success, came to pay their respects.

After the festivities, we met at a bar to mourn. As usual for such a gathering, our stories were told and old lies were relived. In my friends' collective memories, we were more wild, crazy and courageous than I could recall.

With the subject of bad behavior broached, more tales of shameful acts and woeful deeds were to follow. Bobby suggested we all reveal the one transgression that we were the most ashamed of.

What was spoken could have come from the activities log of Sodom and Gomorrah. Tales of desperation and debauchery were mixed with those of bedevilment and betrayal. Jerry was the last to reveal.

We all expected the bar to be raised when Jerry took the stage. He was the one fresh out of jail. By the standards of decent society, Jerry is a bad man.

He took a sip from his beer and began without hesitation. You could tell that he had thought about his answer.

"The worst thing I've ever done, I did to Jimmy Sullivan."

I think we all assumed Jimmy Sullivan was a criminal competitor, prison snitch or cellmate.

"He was in my fourth-grade class," Jerry continued. "His family was real poor and lived in a ratty trailer near the dump. Jim was a mousy little kid with bad teeth. He wore the same clothing to school everyday. His clothes were always clean, but always the same pair of brown pants and blue plaid shirt."

Jerry paused and ran a finger over the scar on his face, then continued.

"One day at recess, in front of a bunch of other kids, I called him Sully-Same-Shirt and it stuck. From then on, no one used his real name—from then on he was Sully-Same-Shirt. I can still remember his face the first time he heard me say that. He actually winced like he had been gut-punched. That look still haunts me.

"I can only imagine the dread he felt as he put on that shirt every morning, having nothing else to wear and knowing the taunts that would follow. He moved away a couple of years later. I never told him I was sorry."

His story was a letdown for all of us. We had anticipated a prison fight, vengeful retaliation or a deal gone sour. What we got was a recount of a schoolyard teasing. No one complained. None of us wanted to replace "Sully-Same-Shirt" as Jerry's worst deed.

It is easy to assume that if you obey the law you're a worthy person. Laws change with society's sensibilities. What is acceptable and legal today can be redone with the sweep of a politico's pen.

The laws of decency are less flexible. A decent person is kind, thoughtful and considerate of others' feelings. By that definition, many, myself included, fall miserably short.

The fact that Jerry felt less guilt for the deeds that put him in prison than he did for his childhood crimes against Sully-Same-Shirt interested me. After all those years, a thoughtless act on the playground plagues him. Sometimes it takes the words of a former convict to remind decent society that being a good citizen does not necessarily make you a good person.

~~~

IF THE BOOZE DOSEN'T KILL YOU, THE JOB WILL

Summit Daily News, 2003

Sure, the Wolfman had a drinking problem, but that was during a time in the early seventies — a time when society was more forgiving of self-abuse.

I met Steve Turner on Cape Cod. I was a member of a transient tribe that worked the ski resorts of Colorado in the winter and the East Coast beaches for the summer and fall seasons.

His nickname was well earned. His hair was long and scraggily. His sphinx-like beard jutted below a set of canine teeth. He was a prep cook and I was the waiter at a large resort. He'd hide his booze in a steak sauce bottle, and after a long night he would offer me a swig with the words, "Go forward Biffy, but never go straight."

Even at that early time in my life, I knew the Wolfman had a problem. But it wasn't to save him that I moved him into my house. It was more just to punish my roommate Keith. When it came to securing rent money from Keith, there was only a small window of opportunity between the time he cashed his paycheck and the time he spent all his money. Sometimes the window was a few days, sometimes a few hours. Invariably, I typically paid all the bills and collected a few bucks at a time.

The Wolfman had been living in his car, which had no engine. When autumn arrived and he was looking for warmer accommodations, I told the Wolfman he could sleep with Keith. It's better to be owed money by two dead beats—at least I was twice as likely to collect.

Keith had taken off for a long weekend and had left no money for rent. When the Wolfman offered me cash for a month's lodging, I jumped at the bird in the hand. There was already an extra bed in Keith's room and he wasn't around to protest, so I told our new roomie to make himself comfortable.

Keith returned two days later in the middle of the night.

"What is that thing in my room?" He asked, shaking me awake violently.

He looked scared.

"That's the Wolfman," I answered simply. "He had money."

"Have you seen how he sleeps?" said Keith.

"No."

"Would you like to?" my friend persisted.

"If I say no, will you let me go back to sleep?" I asked.

"No!"

I got up and walked to Keith's room. Sitting next to a perfectly made bed with his back against the wall was the Wolfman. His eyes were wide open and his pupils rolled back so only the whites showed. He issued a high-pitched, gurgle on intake, coupled with a plaintive, asthmatic wheeze on exhale. I had to admit, at first glance the scene was absolutely frightening. I was glad he wasn't sleeping with me.

"Why is he in my bedroom?" my best friend inquired.

"We only have a month left on our lease, and like I said, he had money."

A compromise was reached: Keith would sleep with me that night and the next day we would relocate the Wolfman to the den.

When I asked the Wolfman if he would mind using our parlor as his bedroom, he acted like we were doing him a favor.

Without a TV, we found our nightly entertainment in watching the Wolfman sleep. We would return home after working late to find a wheezing, cadaverous apparition sitting in our den. It was better than watching The Twilight Zone. The Wolfman could sleep through anything, and occasionally Keith would hang paper clips from his hair, ears and beard like Christmas ornaments.

A few years ago, when they told me that Steve the Wolfman had died, I was not surprised. Almost all of my friends from that era who didn't get healthy quick…got old fast. As the news trickled in from Keith and various sources, it was clear that the Wolfman had died of a heart attack. And it turned out that he had died a rich man. Apparently, Steve had cleaned up, found God, got sober, got married, had kids and sold real estate. From burnout hippie to workaholic yuppie, the change had been dramatic. Prescription drugs and sobriety had all but eliminated his asthma, but work and stress created weight and heart problems. Steve had essentially worked himself to death.

While I'm grateful the Wolfman finally overcame his demons, it's sad that Steve had picked up some new bad habits that killed them both…

~~~

BAD FASHION, GOOD MEAT

Summit Daily News, November 2004

Ernie is very generous with his meat. After only a few rather obvious hints from me, he'll share the fruits of his most recent hunting efforts. As a person who only eats meat once or twice a month, I try to get the stuff that hasn't been pumped with antibiotics and hormones. Although it is possible to buy organic beef at the grocery store, it is much more affordable to get it for free from Ernie.

I mention Ernie's meat to illustrate the fact that I'm not against hunting. As I said, I occasionally eat animals and often wear leather boots, clothing and undergarments.

But I am not a hunter. My experience when encountering wildlife in the backcountry would be diminished if I were to kill it. That said, I understand why harvesting game keeps the species stronger; and surely, it's more humane than how we raise and kill our domestic beef.

Maybe if sport hunting had a catch-and-release policy like fishing, I could get into it. But that would probably have to be more like shoot and transplant. I would hunt and carry spare internal organs in my pack so that after I've blasted one out of a creature I'd quickly perform a heart or kidney transplant and send the critter on its way.

The bottom line is that I don't disapprove of hunting, hunters or free meat. What is disturbing is the heavy-handed pressure I've noticed towards us non-hunters to cover ourselves from head to toe in blaze orange when we recreate on our public lands during deer and elk season.

Over the past few months, while hiking, running and biking from Idaho to Martha's Vineyard, Massachusetts (believe it or not, a hunting destination), we've been lectured about the fact that we were not dressed in acid-pumpkin colors. Let's face it: blaze orange is ugly. Other than for hunters, highway workers and birth control, it has no aesthetic or practical purpose.

Most recently, I was running on a popular trail just outside of Vernal, Utah. When I returned to the trailhead, I encountered a truckload of hunters unloading their ATVs. We said our hellos and all was pleasant, until one surly guy gazed at my black pants and white shirt and said, "You shouldn't be running around here without blaze orange. This is hunting season."

I quickly responded to the guy that unless he was hunting penguins or nuns, my black and white ensemble wasn't a target that any good hunter could confuse with something legal to shoot.

To their credit, his friends laughed. That one guy just scowled.

This same scenario has played out again and again during our national travels. I even got it from non-hunters who stopped us on the trail to warn us of the presence of hunters. Granted I'm not a hunter, but if I were I would scout an area, look for signs, come back during the season, track my quarry, and only pull the trigger once I was sure I had a clean and safe shot. I'm assuming most hunters do just that. So I don't see why anyone should be overly concerned about sharing our public lands. I don't think non-hunters should recreate in fear, and I certainly don't think hunters should ex-pect the rest of us to dress a certain way so they don't shoot us. During the season, I do wear whatever bright clothing I own, but I don't feel compelled to augment my wardrobe.

As long as hunters suffer from the misconception that anything not wearing orange is fair game, the backcountry will be a more dangerous place.

Yes, I mentioned a couple times already that I do not hunt. But I do own the weaponry. Whether I'm shooting at the range or just plinking silhouette targets of the New York Yankees in the woods, I know it is my responsibility to not place anyone in danger by being certain of where my rounds are heading. Expecting the general public to dress in a certain way on our public lands to keep from getting accidentally shot is akin to drunk drivers suggesting other drivers stay off the highways for a few hours after last call.

If hunters, as required by law, want to wear orange then so be it. For the rest of us, we should be able to dress as we please without compromising our safety. I say it again, the only person who looks good in that color is Ernie and that is only when he is reaching in his freezer…

~~~

FROM UGLY DUCKLING TO GOLFING SWAN

Vail Daily News, 2004

I have no idea how Michael Franks got to where he is today. But I do know where he began. In a middle-class neighborhood filled with the poor and unremarkable, Michael Franks stood out for having little going for him. Raised by a single mother—and one mean mother of a mother at that—and a sadistic half brother, Michael didn't need the physical deformities he was born with to set him apart.

In retrospect, I can see that Mrs. Franks' maliciousness was probably due to stress and sleep deprivation, but from the eyes of a child, she was simply "The Witch" to us kids in the neighborhood. Although she labored through the graveyard shift in a shoe factory, she always seemed quite awake in the middle of the day while screaming at us: "Quiet down! Play somewhere else!"

There was no Mr. Franks, which was an added embarrassment for Michael. It was one thing to have a "dead father" or "a father in jail," but to simply have "no father" was the worst.

Whoever Michael's father was, the man cursed his son with a mess of bad genes. Michael was doomed with a leg several inches shorter than the other and a bony misshapen head. I honestly don't recall if Michael was smart, funny or creative. All that I can recall is that he waved his shortcomings like a flag.

I can picture him now limping around the bases, dragging his short leg, and three-inch-thick soled shoe with a determined demeanor. He was always the last to be picked in football games; he was saddled with unflattering nicknames like Pegleg and Snaggletooth; and he was generally taunted, even by his half brother Jackie.

This produced in Michael a way of making himself unnoticed. He walked with his head down and spoke in mumbled tones. When teased he surrendered, and when struck he covered up. He seemed to take comfort in being ignored and overlooked. Because when you're overlooked, you're not being directly abused.

When we reached our teenage years, the kids from my neighborhood were bused to a school on the other side of town. The only memory I have of Michael during the high school years was of our homeroom teacher telling him — announcing so all could hear — that due to "his condition," he was excused from gym. While the rest of us were making new friends, meeting girls and playing sports, Michael hid.

I tell you what I know of Michael's story because of the strange way he was brought back into my life many years later in a bar by some friends returning from a Florida vacation. They had strolled in sporting fresh golf tans, Hawaiian shirts and rat ears (Disney

World was also a stop), and told tales of birdies, bogies and drunken Disney rides. I feigned interest, knowing that there would be no slide show to follow. In the middle of a story involving debauchery on the fairway, my friend John handed me a business card. "We met this guy at the country club. He says he used to know you."

The card read Michael Franks, MBA, Financial Advisor, Manager. It was printed on the thick stock paper of a large, well-known brokerage house.

When I asked my friends to describe Michael's appearance and demeanor, they all agreed that Michael was your typical, well-dressed country clubber, a good golfer, confident and good-natured. I inquired again of his appearance, but they were vague. The best I could gather was that he had appeared successful and walked with just a slight limp.

They couldn't recall who or how my name was mentioned — it seemed all three were sober enough to have only uncertain recollections of that day. They did say that after Michael made the connection, he handed them his card and said, "Give this to Biff." My buddy Joey made the observation that he seemed proud of that card. As I walked home that night in the dark, I had a wonderful sense of elation, knowing that two thousand miles away someone whom I had watched suffer had overcome all odds to find happiness...

~~~

CHANGING A LIFE ON A CHAIR LIFT

Backcountry Magazine, November 2002

I ruined a young girl's life last week. It was her fault; she trusted me.

She was young, naive, and angelic and had just graduated with a theology degree. Her red hair framed a boyish face. She called me Sir. We were stuck on a stalled chair lift, and as it is often the case when strangers meet with an assumption of never meeting again, there was nothing for us to lose in being completely honest with one another. She told me she was visiting her girlfriend who lived and worked in the mountains. And she was scheduled to return home to Indiana the next day. She mentioned a boyfriend carried over from high school, and a religious family who said grace before every meal—even breakfast.

She was as happy as only a young girl set free can be. The last seven days had been the best week of her life. She loved the mountains, loved to snowboard, and even claimed to feel closer to God at ten thousand feet. Her girlfriend offered her a place to live and a job if she would stay for the rest of the season. But that would mean disappointing her father and boyfriend. She admitted that if she stayed, she was afraid she would never leave. "It just feels right here," she said.

She made two mistakes that day. First, she was truthful to a stranger; then she asked my opinion.

It was one of those perfect ski days. Deep snow, no crowds, clear skies. A day that served to reaffirm our choices. I had spent the day powder skiing and eating chocolate-covered espresso beans for nutrition and energy. The beans dilate your pupils and leave black specks on your teeth. I must have appeared to be a speed freak badly in need of dental hygiene. So as the chair lift swung in the wind, I waxed fanatically like a hyperactive, black-toothed coal miner.

If she was hoping to find a voice of reason in the hedonistic world of a resort community, she might have looked to someone else. I'm a firm believer in tailoring your career to suit your geographic desires. In other words, decide where you want to be and what makes you happy, and then find a job that allows you the ability to enjoy both. I've always felt that work is a means to an end — the end being quality of life. I suppose I might have tempered my declarations as a concession to knowing little about her, but I was buzzed.

And so I rambled: "Indiana is a trap. Your parents, boyfriend, career are all pits filled with punji-sticks of boredom. If you go back, you'll be regretting what you did for the rest of your life. You'll grow old and die without ever having lived."

"You can start with a clean slate here," I added, mentioning that often when living in a new place there are no preconceived notions existing in regards to who you are and what you're like.

That seemed to appeal to her. "I'm tired of being a good girl," she said. "I want to get a tattoo."

I thought that was a great idea, and I suggested she take up drinking as well.

I know, I know… I have my biases. In retrospect, she had caught me at a moment when my caffeine and powder rush was peaking. I was beyond any understanding of why anyone would choose to live any other way than this. If I had spoken to her after a bad day at work or during another spring break when my neighbors in the next condo are as drunk as pigs and as old as my clothing, I might have had a more realistic assessment of resort life. But right then, I was high, happy and convinced. What works for me, might not work for this young girl, but I offered my opinions as if they were Scripture. (Come on, opinions are like nose hair, we all have them.) And she bought it.

By the time we reached the top and said our good-byes, she was ready to call Dad, and her Dude, and tell them not to hold dinner for her. As I skied away, I was feeling pretty good about myself. I felt like a preacher of the Gospel of Good Times, and I had found another convert. The euphoria of saving a young girl from a life I would find boring set me aglow. It wasn't until I got home and the beans wore off that I realized I might have spoken too soon. All I knew about that little girl was the little she told me. In one chair lift ride, I might have broken a daddy's heart, ruined a relationship and done damage to a promising career. I felt awful.

So this story is my attempt at making it all right. If that redheaded girl from Muncie, Indiana is reading this, I have one more thing to say: "Before you move to the mountains or get that tattoo, you might consider getting a second opinion. Just don't ask someone from the flatlands, they might not understand…"

~~~

REALITY IS NOT ALL IT IS CRACKED UP TO BE

Summit Daily News, January 2001

Ed rolled over in the tent. He looked at me and spoke.

"Sometimes, I wake up and forget I'm paralyzed."

I nodded and asked, "How does it feel when you remember?"

"By the time I remember I can't walk," he said. "I remember that it could be worse. But in the meantime, I enjoy the hell out of the possibilities."

Ed Baker was a South Georgia redneck. He served two tours of duty in Vietnam and returned home without a scratch. He fell in love, married and was nearly killed in a logging accident. His marriage fell apart a month after his spinal cord did.

I met Ed Baker almost ten years ago. I had spent most of the spring watching my mother die of lung cancer. Since I didn't feel very funny that summer, I decided to take some time off from my comedian job to work for a handicap outdoor program. Ed and I were part of a group of ten—some blind, some crippled, some crazy—on a seven-day canoe trip through the Canadian wilderness. We'd paddle from lake to lake carrying our boats, gear and, sometimes, our passengers over land bridges up to two miles long. Often, two of the able-bodied would hoist a wheelchair with its occupant while simultaneously leading a sightless camper over steep, rocky portages. My two fellow guides were well trained and competent. My credentials were that I could afford to work cheap and made for amusing campfire conversation.

Ed spent much of his time inside a self-created reality. He called the place between sleep and consciousness, fantasy and fact, his "tweener-times." He claimed the beauty of tweener-time was that he was alert enough to desire and asleep enough to dream, thus all things were possible. He told me how he'd try to hover on the edge of slumber as long as possible and create a better life. He would go into great detail of the situation he invented. First and foremost, he was out of that wheelchair, but he also was married to a girl he met only once in Okinawa, and he was once again able to hunt.

"I swear Biff, sometimes I can hold onto my tweener-time long enough to run through the woods until my feet hurt or smell my wife's skin. It is so real, I sometimes don't know what to believe, my dead legs or the imaginary blisters on my toes."

At the time, I wasn't open-minded enough to appreciate Ed's survival instinct. Instead, he began to creep me out. I was afraid he would dream of me as an albino Vietcong reclining next to him and hit me on the head with a rock. I began sleeping with one eye open.

I don't know if Ed's "tweener" obsession was psychologically healthy or not. I do know it seemed to give him an incredible amount of pleasure. Other than his physical challenges, rebel flag tattoo and his love for The Dukes of Hazzard television show, he seemed a normal and happy person. My guess was that his fantasy life was a harmless diversion and escape. It has been my experience that reality has room for interpretation.

The difference between joy and depression is often perception. In other words, happiness is less about your situation than it is how about how you perceive your situation. In Dante's Divine Comedy, written on the gates of hell are the words, "All hope abandon, ye who enter here!" The message plainly is that pain without hope is pure horror.

A couple of years before he died, I interviewed Superman, Christopher Reeves. I was amazed and inspired by his strength and determination. He was speaking of recent advancements in spinal cord research and urging the government to provide more funding. Near the end of our visit, I asked if he believed it possible that he might walk again. His answer was an emphatic "Yes." Though other experts in that field were less optimistic, given his determination, I believed him.

Ed and Mr. Reeves had more than a wheelchair in common. They were able to envision a life for themselves that many others say is impossible. One relied on faith in science, the other cultivated a mental state void of the negative. And both had learned to make the best of a seemingly unendurable circumstance. The fact that Reeves did not walk again might be less important than the strong will he adapted while he was living. Likewise, Ed's tweener-time was so much more than an attempt to escape the inevitable reality of his situation. When it came to his contentment, the ends most always justify the means. Whatever it takes to bring

pleasure and provide hope should be chased and sa-
vored…

~~~

UNTIL DEATH DO US PART

Summit Daily News, September 2004

The last time I spoke to Robert he had just finished
changing his wife's diaper. He told me this with no
trace of self-pity, but rather to share one of the remaining intimacies of a couple still very much in love.

Although the cancer had ravaged Mary's body and
bowels, she remained the object of Robert's constant
affection. She learned of her cancer on her forty-third
birthday. With drugs and determination she fought the
good fight, but eventually the disease would prove
stronger than science. As recently as last spring, they
spoke with optimism of her chances. That confidence
diminished with every setback and pound lost; all
Robert could do was try his best to keep her comfortable.

Robert is a successful jazz musician. (If I were to use
his real name, more than a few of you would recognize
it.) Mary is only famous for being Bob's mate. But
those who knew her well (unfortunately, I'm not one of
them) claim she had a near clairvoyant intuition and a
saint-like kindness that even overshadowed Robert's
genius.

They met over twenty years ago in New York City.
Robert was playing horn in the Village, and Mary was

a hostess at a popular after-hours restaurant. She was unique that night, both a Spanish beauty and uninterested in the dashing musician. He flirted. She was coy. He persisted. She resisted. When he asked her on a date, she told him to ask her again when he wasn't living in a hotel.

The music took Robert all over the world during the next five years. When he returned to the city, Mary still greeted guests at the restaurant, but now she owned the place. They dated, fell in love and moved in together.

Mary ran their lives with the same cordial efficiency that she ran her restaurant. Robert was blessed with his music, but when it came to organizing his life, he was a mess. She paid the bills, kept their calendar and made sure her husband dressed well on stage. Robert's manager would call Mary first to run the performance dates by her before he even approached her mate.

When Robert was frail and temperamental, Mary was a rock of health and stability. She sold her restaurant, which gave her more time to manage Robert's life and career, and together they flourished.

It is ironic that Robert, the sensitive, artistic hypochondriac, ten years Mary's senior, would be the one called upon as caregiver. But he more than rose to the occasion. As Mary's health deteriorated Robert remained home with her. He became the one to run their home and kept visitors from tiring his wife.

I was never in their inner circle, but I kept up on Mary's condition through mutual friends. I allowed myself one phone call every few months, but that faded to just short e-mails.

By all reports, Robert seldom left her side. Even with a live-in housekeeper and hospice nurse, Robert preferred to perform the more delicate and often unpleasant tasks himself. He said to a friend of mine, "She is as beautiful dying as she was when she first broke my heart in the East Village".

Mary and Robert were never legally married. It never seemed important. With the likelihood of Mary's death, the reality of their common law situation became evident. Financially, it was only a minor inconvenience; when Mary first got sick, she signed her assets over to her lover. But being life partners instead of a married couple opened a Pandora's box of concern. Some hospitals allow only family members to visit patients in intensive care. Robert would not be able to take possession of her remains for burial. And most importantly, during what surely will be the most difficult time in his life, the state afforded him no rights that would normally be given to a spouse. It is as if caring for, living with and loving each other for nearly twenty years meant nothing.

The sensible thing to do would have been for Mary and Robert to get a Justice of the Peace to come to her bedside and marry them. That would certainly have solved some problems. If Mary's last hours were in a hospital, Robert could be by her side. And when the inevitable occurred, he could manage her estate with fewer lawyers involved. If nothing else a marriage certificate would validate the love and devotion that this couple enjoyed and the suffering and sacrifice they endured.

Robert and Mary cannot get married. Our government won't let them.

Truth be told, there is no Robert and Mary—just Robert and Martin. Our president, our governor and many of our other leaders don't recognize the sanctity of same sex unions. They are doing all they can to prevent same sex couples from being allowed to marry. They contend that the only sacred marriage is one between a man and a woman. They say this even though half of all heterosexuals' marriages end in separation or divorce.

I wouldn't want to tell Robert that his relationship with Martin was not sacred. I would especially not want to tell him that after he sat up all night with his mate cleaning, caring and watching him slowly die. I would rather tell him that love, not gender, makes a union sacred.

~~~

ROTTEN SNOW AND A PAINFUL MEMORY

Backcountry Magazine, December 2003

Greta looked to be in her sixties. She was round, jolly, German and stoned on white wine and pain pills. The Riesling was from the refrigerator in her RV; I provided the Vicoden.

We met her at a campground in southern Colorado, in late May. My mate and I were out on our yearly search for spring snow. We called it "Corn Camp," but on this trip we found more mashed potatoes than corn. The unusually warm evening temperatures were a source of much frustration and complaints. We'd ski off the summits on good snow only to face endless sections of leg-breaking jump-turns in knee-deep slop all the way back to the trailhead.

A double-heel-release head plant had brought my face and ski tips together, producing a golf ball sized knot on my forehead, which I was treating with a can of beer and bag of semi-frozen peas when Greta first walked past the camper. Robby, our small tail-wagging Terrier, ran to her and tried to impregnate her shoes. She called him "little Liebchen" (that's German for dog-child of Satan) and bent over to scratch him behind the ears. A cute dog is an icebreaker. What would normally appear to be two unwashed ski-bums, with burnt faces, pale bodies and black toenails, suddenly transform into respectable people if they have a lovable cur.

After the usual small talk—"What a cute dog," "It's nearly summer, did you really ski today?" "You're married? I thought she was your daughter!"—Greta invited us over to her RV for wine and hors d'oeuvres. Since our dinner menu that night consisted of beer, instant oatmeal and Clif Bars, we accepted. We warned her that we were very hungry and promised to do the dishes. She insisted that the meal and dishes would be her treat, but asked if we had any aspirin for her sprained ankle. I told her I could do a little better than that, and we'd be back over in twenty minutes. I'm no doctor, but I am a hypochondriac. I always keep a few mild narcotics in my travel kit in case of imaginary injuries.

By the time we arrived, she had laid out cheese, sausage and crackers. There was wine chilling and a Wagner disk on the CD player. Appetizers turned into dinner, and Wagner into polka music, and a second bottle of wine was opened. Greta was limping slightly on an ankle that looked swollen and sprained. I told her, in my opinion, taking an aspirin for an injury such as hers would be like spitting on a forest fire; I recommended something stronger and cut a Vicoden in half. I was worried that I might have prescribed an underdose when Greta began to yodel.

Somewhere between hors d'oeuvres and yodels we had switched from small talk to the heavy truths. We traded life stories. Ellen and I told of our upbringings, old loves, past indiscretions. Greta spoke of the husbands and boyfriends she dumped and outlived. She talked of girlhood in Germany and migration to America. When I asked her if she remembered much from the Second World War, she said she remembered only one thing. This is the story she told.

The war hit civilians hard in Germany. Rationing of the short supply of basic goods and comforts was widespread. A week before Christmas, her elderly father borrowed a horse and cart and took Greta, age six, and her younger sister on what he called a "secret mission." They headed into the country and eventually came to a small farmhouse. As they approached, Greta became aware of the most wonderful smell. They walked in on an old woman stirring a huge pot of chocolate over an open fire. Displayed on a table were assorted sweets and candies. Each sister was allowed to pick three treats, which were wrapped in tissue paper and not to be opened until Christmas.

The ride home found the two girls sitting in the cart staring in rapture at wrapped candy on their laps. Greta's mouth watered in anticipation of Christmas morning. Their father warned them if they saw soldiers to hide the treats. "I bought sweets for my two favorite girls, not for some sweaty cannon fodder."

The sun was setting when they crossed railroad tracks on which rested an empty boxcar with a broken axle listing dramatically to one side. The boxcar was obviously jettisoned by the locomotive that would later return with a new container to retrieve the contents. Next to the tracks was a fenced enclosure. Inside were gaunt, frightened children, too many to count—some were crying. Outside, a few soldiers lingered. One sauntered over and curtly suggested they move along; no mention was made of the pen or the occupants.

The road continued next to the fence line for fifty yards. Before it turned off, the old man stopped the wagon to check the horse's feet. While he did so, he whispered urgently for his daughters to throw the chocolates over the fence to the children. The girls resisted, yet eventually with tears of confusion and frustration, they tossed their Christmas sweets over the fence to the hollow-eyed children. As they drove away, a young boy waved and smiled.

"That's all I remember of the war, but I remember it well because I'm reminded of that smile in my dreams."

As Ellen and I walked to our camper late that evening the temperature felt to be well over fifty degrees. We knew that the next day's skiing was going to be somewhere between marginal and rotten. Normally that would be a cause for complaint, but on this night we simply felt grateful to be well fed and free to live as we chose.

~~~

TAKE A WALK ON THE WEIRD SIDE

Summit Daily News, April 2003

Lazara is a witch doctor.

When I say witch doctor, I don't mean a gynecologist who makes house calls on a broom. Rather, Lazara is a medicine man—he has some powers that defy logic and explanation. He calls himself a shaman, which he described as a human with a connection between the natural and supernatural. I simply say he's spooky.

I met Lazara about fifteen years ago. He was in Colorado for a series of lectures and workshops that he was giving around the state. The event's promoter called and asked if this shaman could appear on a television show I was hosting to publicize the events.

I arrived for the taping in a petulant mood. My demeanor was worsened after I was told that my guest was running late and I'd have no time to speak to him before his interview. Normally this wouldn't be that big of an issue, but I did not want to be there and was surly about it. In truth, I wanted to be in Boston attending the funeral of my old friend Rudy.

Why Rudy had killed himself is not important to this story. It's sufficient to say he was burdened with guilt and depression. He left behind a mother, brother and lover, all of whom I knew well. I had looked into rescheduling my work obligations in order to leave town and attend his service, but I could not do so without inconveniencing many people; not the least of whom was myself. So I was forced to honor my commitments and curse myself for it.

I was more than halfway through the hour show when Lazara was led into the studio. His appearance was striking. He had long blonde hair, wore leather pants and vest, his prominent nose and high cheekbones suggested a Native American heritage but with fair-skinned Teutonic coloring. We had only a few minutes to talk as they put on his microphone and the commercials played. When we went to air, he began to speak in a quiet voice. He ignored the cameras and looked straight into my eyes for the entire length our talk. When the interview was over, we shook hands and he stood up to leave. At that moment, I still wasn't sure if he was truly who he said he was or a charismatic, new age conman. As he left, he walked over to a cameraman named Scott, put his hand on Scott's shoulder and whispered in his ear. They both looked at me, and my co-worker nodded.

The rest of the hour was non-eventful. I was getting up to leave, when Scott walked over and said, "Dude, this is weird. Did someone you know just die?"

I had not mentioned Rudy's passing to anyone at work. In fact, with the exception of my girlfriend, I hadn't mentioned it to anyone.

I asked Scott, "How do you know that?"

His eyes bulged behind his wire-framed glasses when he said, "Dude, I knew it, that guy creeped me out. Look." Scott rolled up his sleeves and his arms were covered with goose bumps.

"Calm down," I said. "What are you talking about?"

"Dude, I'm freaked, when that guy touched me I tingled all over. I swear Dude, I almost wet myself."

My bad mood was beginning to return. "Scott, what are you talking about? What did he say?"

"He told me to tell you to stop feeling guilty, there is nothing you can do for your friend now. He told me to tell you that your friend's pain has ended and he is in a better place."

I am nearly positive that the Shaman was not told of Rudy's death by any human source. I can only explain his knowledge as unexplainable. When I told this story to a Christian friend, he said that the Shaman works for the Devil. I don't buy that.

There are some things and some people that are beyond the grasp of a meat-and-potatoes guy, like myself. That doesn't make them evil or sacrilegious, only incomprehensible. For me, any viable proof of a world beyond this one, be it from a pastor, priest or witch doctor, is a comfort. Since the dawn of mankind's time, what we cannot explain we either worship or condemn. I'm certainly not going to denounce Lazara, lest he turn me into a toad. Yet I'm not ready to add his name on my list to worship. I'm very comfortable with the fact that there is much about this life and the next that I don't understand. Unfortunately by the time all my questions are answered, I won't be around to share the information. But that's okay.

I'd hate to live in a world without mystery.

CHAPTER 4: DEAD PEOPLE

Every one of you who reads this chapter will someday be dead. The people featured in it already are.

"THAT HE NOT BUSY BEING BORN, IS BUSY DYING"–Bob Dylan

Various Colorado Papers, *March 2001*

(This story was written over the course of twenty months before it was completed.)

I stood in the crowd and watched him play his guitar.

I was dancing (what I call dancing) and was surrounded by friends. Most of us in the room knew that John was very sick. And we knew that it was only a matter of time before cancer would finally accomplish what blindness, disease and hardship could not—but they could not wipe the smile off John's face. I think we all had the feeling that we would remember this night.

I left that bar two hours ago, it is now two a.m. I'm typing drunk. Watching him tonight, I felt both great grief and respect. Grief knowing it would be a miracle if John lived another two years. Respect because the man on stage had managed to entertain us despite his intense pain. I know, first hand, how hard it is to entertain when suffering from things as little as a bad mood, head cold or a sore back. I can only imagine the courage it takes to stand on stage playing music and telling bad jokes after your doctors have given you a sooner-than-later death prognosis. There was a moment during the chorus of a John Prine song when I saw his face convulse in a tremor of pain. I fought back the tears and looked for a waitress. It was hard to see him like that, but I wasn't sure if I'd get another chance to hear him play. So I did what we emotional Irish cripples have been doing for generations—I drank a fair amount of whiskey.

My livelihood for years has been to take my real life experiences, often involving friends and family, and share them in my columns and television and radio shows. Sometimes, I feel that I make my living just by living. I'll sit on this story in hopes that John's recovery will turn it into fiction.

When I met him twenty years ago, John was one of the best blind athletes on the planet. He competed and won Nordic races all over the world against highly subsidized athletes. I, too, was a cross-country ski racer, often winning the "convicted felon, talk-show host with a speech impediment" category at regional races.

It was at that time that I began to guide John through some of his competitions and workouts. I would ski in front, next to or behind him and describe the terrain and suggest technique. We skied together in a few open races, and John beat many of the sighted skiers while I struggled to keep up. What I remember most was John's joy, enthusiasm, and courage. He fearlessly caromed down narrow, tree-lined trails on the brink of control. I'd be screaming directions and John would simply scream.

When ski-guiding the blind, a guide's last resort is to yell, "SIT!" That signals to the skier that he is in danger and must immediately sit or fall to stop before hitting something or someone. There were times when the speed with which John managed to weave through the trees over an icy trail made me very uncomfortable. Not wanting to be responsible for ending his competitive career—or life—I'd yell, "SIT," and sometimes John would refuse. At the bottom of the hill, John would be howling with delight.

"Damnit, John," I'd say. "You've got to sit when I make the call.

John would look at me and say, "Oh, were you talking to me?"

***

John has already fought two rounds with cancer and won. By all accounts this last bout should have killed him. I know he is sick, scared and hurting; I've never heard him complain.

He was on stage that night singing "Bobby Magee." He belted out the line, "Freedom's just another word for nothing left to lose." My emotions swamped me and I was glad for the Crown Royal in my hand. As the packed room swayed to John's music, I noticed that most people displayed what I like to call a contradiction of expressions—many had tears in their eyes and a smile on their face. Anyone who can make you laugh and cry at the same time is a remarkable person.

***

I recently learned that John hasn't long to live. Although he's beaten the odds of a diagnosis like this before, it looks far grimmer now. Up to a few days ago, he was still able to ignore the pain, play some music and tell bad jokes. Truth in journalism requires me to point out that the cancer didn't damage John's comedic delivery — it never was very good. He continues to perform, only much less often and for shorter periods of time.

It's possible that John will do what few have managed to do and beat his condition. It's possible that he'll read this column and chide me for my usual habit of overreacting. Or maybe in this incidence, unlike times past, when God tells my friend to "SIT" John will finally obey.

~~~

A COLD DEATH AND WARM MEMORIES

Backcountry Magazine, December 2004

Tim looked peacefully asleep. But we knew he was dead.

Only moments before, his closest friends had dug his body out from nearly ten feet of snow. This was almost twenty years ago, but I still remember the look on the faces of friends and family as we lifted his body out of the pit. Mixed in with the near unbearable grief, there was fear — the fear that our own futures were in peril if someone so young, healthy and backcountry savvy could die such a death.

To make matters worse, he was just the first of three bodies we would find that day. The other two belonged to Steve and his dog, Jackson.

The resort town in which I live was a much smaller place then. When these well-known members of the community didn't come home after the day of back-country skiing, it was only natural that all who knew them would join in on the search. Around those three holes were a dozen friends, relatives, lovers and roommates. It was the first and last time I saw most of them cry.

That day, for many, marked the first experience of losing someone young and close. Not me. I remember thinking, we've found them, now what? Part of me wanted to re-bury Tim, Steve and Jackson, and just pretend they were still missing.

Eulogies make heroes of us all. Seldom will an obituary read: "Joe Blow died last week. He had the morals of a cockroach and was as ugly as a bucket of nose hairs." It is natural in our grief to reconstruct the deceased in terms that are bigger than life and truth. This is a good thing; nothing is served with posthumous reality.

The true test of a person's greatness is the legacy they leave behind.

Without falling prey to the temptation of maudlin exaggeration, I'd say that Tim McClure was a remarkable man. Though the years have lent some perspective to his accomplishments and qualities, by all accounts he was a visionary. Tim created a recycling program in the mid-seventies, when few in this country knew what the term meant. There is a national award that bears his name.

He was the first person I knew that free-heeled on short fat skis—160cm alpine rental skis—and old leather ski-jumping boots, wore an avalanche transceiver and made his own probes out of tent poles. He was both a pacifist and state-wrestling champion. Unimpressed by wealth and authority, he was equally comfortable drinking a beer with the Mayor and District Attorney, as well as guys named Wacky Tim and Dirty Mike.

I just returned from the yearly fund-raising banquet to benefit the county's recycling program. Though the event is named for Tim, most in attendance never knew him. Yet interspersed among the hundreds present, I saw several of those who were there when we found their bodies. It's funny, in a community where hundreds come and go yearly, most of us who were there that day in 1985 have made the mountains our home. In my mind's eye, we all appear much the same as we did that day we mourned over the lifeless pits in the snowfield.

I visit the sight where we found our friends several times a year. I go not so much as a pilgrimage, but simply because it is a wonderful place to run, bike and ski. Every time I'm there alone, I call out to my missing friends. So far no one has answered. We often like to assume that the spirit of those lost stays where they took their last breath. But, in truth, this place is merely a grave. It's within the essence of all who knew them where their spirit and memory remains...

~~~

LIVING A LIFE THAT MAKES FOR A GOOD OBITUARY

Various Colorado Papers, *September 2004*

If you want guidance on how to live your life, you should try to write your own obituary. The rational: How you would like to be remembered is how you ought to live.

Jeffrey Bergeron, alias Biff America, aka Pudding Drawers, Fudge Undies and Turkey Neck, died last Tuesday of natural causes. He was one hundred and six years old. Up to the end of his life, Bergeron/America retained his sense of humor and most of his hair. He will be remembered for his poor spelling and love of outdoor recreation.

After a successful stint in the food service industry, Bergeron/America embarked on mediocre yet tumultuous media career. He was awarded a Pulitzer Prize for his exposé of former vice-president Dick Cheney's extramarital affair with Siegfried and Roy. He retired early at the age of fifty-five. This was made possible by a frivolous lawsuit filed against a ski resort for temporary impotence caused by a cold Poma chair.

After receiving a sizable settlement, Mr. America dedicated his life and much of his resources in support of liberal causes and keeping his wife happy. He was active in the Democratic and Green Party as well as various charitable and social causes such as children's welfare, homeless issues and the legalization of medical marijuana.

Even at the end of his life, Bergeron/America was known as a tireless champion of those less fortunate and ecological causes and as a sexual athlete — verification available from his widow upon request.

Bergeron is survived by his wife of sixty-six years, Ellen, who took the day off from powder skiing to attend the second half of his funeral, and by his dog Robby, who died twenty years earlier but was stuffed. In lieu of flowers, donations can be made to the Hillary Clinton Presidential Library.

The beauty of writing your own obit is that it can be a wish list of how you'd like your life to be. Granted, when I wrote my death notice, I took some poetic license in my claims to living one hundred and six years, winning a frivolous lawsuit, being a sexual athlete and retaining most of my hair.

But even if everything else in my faux-obituary is a figment of my fantasies, the part about kindness and compassion does not have to be. Not everyone wins awards, but we can all give something back to mankind and the planet.

I just read a real-life obituary of a man named Nick Vennitucci, the son of an immigrant coal miner. Nick died at the age of ninety-three.

He was a farmer who might have passed through this world unnoticed but for his generosity with pumpkins. One day in the mid 1940s, just before Halloween, Vennitucci stopped his truck on the side of the road and handed out pumpkins to passing school children. This act of kindness must have satisfied him because he continued to do that for over fifty years. As the demand grew, he dedicated twenty-five acres of his farm exclusively for children's pumpkins.

Next to Vennitucci's obituary was one for Fred Ebb. Ebb wrote the lyrics to the Broadway hit "New York,

New York," "Cabaret," "Chicago," and many other Broadway and movie hits. During his life, Ebb won many awards and was regarded as one of the best lyricists of his generation. Though he did great things in his life, I was struck by the fact that Fred Ebb's obituary was half the size of a poor farmer who gave pumpkins to kids.

A sculpture of Vennitucci handing a pumpkin to a child will be erected in front of the Pioneer Museum. In addition to bronze memorial, the uneducated son of an immigrant was venerated by having streets and schools named after him, and honored by then Governor Roy Romer.

I've heard it said that you seldom see a hearse pulling a U-Haul. Had Nick Vennitucci sold those pumpkins instead of giving them away to children, he may have died with more money in the bank. He also would have left the world a lesser place. I would also guess the same spirit that motivated him towards kindness and generosity was part of the reason he lived so long.

After reading about Nick Vennitucci, I have decided to go back and rewrite my own obituary. I'll include more incidences of compassion and consideration and leave out the parts about my Pulitzer and sexual athletics. Because in truth, I probably will never win a Pulitzer Prize and wouldn't want my history of sexual athletics to intimidate my ninety-six year old widow's next husband...

~~~

HEROES OF WAR AND PEACE

Summit Daily News, May 2005

If someone were to take only a quick glance at that photo album, they would have no idea just how much I loved Jeremiah.

The collection of pictures, featuring images of my nephew and me, spans twenty-two years. The shots were gathered, bound in a leather album and given to me about a year after Jeremiah died while serving in the Peace Corps in West Africa. He was killed when his truck rolled over in the Niger desert.

The book was compiled by his mother, my sister.

It begins with a photo taken after his first day of kindergarten.

It shows a young boy in new school clothing being held upside-down by his ankles by a man sporting long hair and a leather jacket. What I found particularly amusing about the photo was the child still clutched what looked to be artwork from his first day of school.

The last picture features a muscular, handsome twenty-something-Jeremiah in a rugby shirt being crowded out of the camera's eye by a man who looks to be an older version of that guy in the leather coat. This time the nephew is much larger than his elder uncle, yet he good-naturedly makes no effort to push back.

Between those two snapshots are nearly a dozen pictures of Jeremiah being placed in headlocks, gentle chokeholds and full nelsons. A few depict a scared boy wearing boxing gloves standing across from an older, bigger boy, wearing gloves and an evil grin.

I thought I'd have a lifetime to show my fondness for my nephew. I hoped he realized how much I loved him even when I had him in a headlock.

Jeremiah was born to a shy, brilliant, mother and an unstable Vietnam-veteran dad.

The marriage lasted less than a decade. My nephew and his sister were left with a mother who worked two jobs and raised her children with much love but very little money. When I was around, I'd spend more time with Jeremiah than his father ever had.

Even as a child, I wasn't really that fond of children. For that reason, I always assumed I'd not reproduce. Since the day he was born, I thought of Jeremiah as the son I'd never have. I knew his father was at best cold and distant and at worst abusive, so I tried to be just the opposite. It wasn't until after he died and I saw all those pictures that I wished my love had been more affectionate and less martial.

Jeremiah graduated from a Catholic high school where he excelled at both sports and scholastics. He won a scholarship to Tulane, graduated and then moved to Colorado. He was a big, handsome and affable lad; he had his mother's sweetness, his uncle's sense of humor and a kindness born from firsthand knowledge of life's cruelties.

Everyone liked Jeremiah.

When he told me he wanted to join the Peace Corps, I told him he was crazy.

I thought he should remain in the mountains and live the life of a self-indulgent ski bum. While I could teach him to box, my sister's son had a difficult time learning the art of selfishness.

We all grieved for Jeremiah, but his death nearly killed his mother.

Though I can honestly say it was one of the most difficult periods in my life, any grief I felt was a fraction of his mother's anguish. She lost not only her first born, but also the only man in her life. Ten years later, my sister still has not come close to recovering—she never will.

I thought of Jeremiah this past Memorial Day when I heard stories on the radio of those who died in America's many wars and the families they left behind.

Although Jeremiah did not perish in battle, my nephew died while serving his country. He traveled to a poor nation to demonstrate America's compassion and greatness in the deserts of Africa.

His death reminded me of the residual misery that is left behind long after a warrior is buried. Thinking of his passing on a day that honors those who have died for causes, good and bad, further cements my resolve to always question the reasons and validity of every instance where our nation sends troops into harm's way. Though all who serve are heroes, they are sent to serve by those who sit safely behind the protective walls of bureaucracy.

Those leaders need to be reminded that they are not only sending troops—they are sending sons and daughters, fathers and mothers. The causes need be just and employed as a last resort.

We must hold fast to the truth that all who make that ultimate sacrifice are worthy of our respect and gratitude. But we must solidly hold to the principal that we will not endanger the life of even one of our most young and innocent to a cause not creditable.

Not only for the sake of those in whose lives are on the line, but for the mothers, fathers, sisters, children and uncles left behind…

~~~

JIMMY'S ASHES

Backcountry Magazine, February 2003

Four years ago, J.B. could never have carried Jimmy to the top of a thirteen-thousand-foot, snow-covered peak. But a lot has happened to Jimmy since then. He was diagnosed with cancer, died and was cremated. In Jimmy's new condensed state, J.B. could have hauled him alone with little difficulty, but he didn't. He thoughtfully portioned out several yogurt-sized containers of Jimmy so a few of us could share the load.

About twenty friends, in various stages of our own personal decay, made the climb on that winter day to celebrate the life of a comrade and to throw his ashes to the wind.

It amazed me that a man, who was so large in the flesh, a former ski patroller, promoter and stonemason, could be carried so easily. It was a reminder that when it is all said and done, after a life of love, pain, boredom and bliss, a man's body is insignificant when compared to his soul. What seemed significant was how many friends—on a day windy enough to blow the tattoo off a snowboarder's forehead—made it to the summit.

There was a simple satisfaction in carrying the remains to a special place without the ritual and expense of the status quo burial. Rather than packaging our comrade in oak and cement and planting him with other dead people, Jimmy's essence would become part of what he loved, a steeply pitched mountain bowl. His ashes would bless and fertilize the tundra; what was not absorbed would be spread by the spring run off. The remains of a man become part of the mountains where that man called home. For the record, that's what I want done. I, too, want to be recycled.

I was raised to believe in a precise and Catholic divine determination of a soul's destination after death. God would examine your life. If you were good, you went to Heaven. If you were bad, you went to Hell, or Fargo. It was a lot like Santa Claus, deciding who's been naughty and who's been nice, but for bigger stakes.

Jimmy couldn't be bothered with divine reckoning. He simply enlisted the services of those who loved him to carry his remains to a place where his soul already was.

By appearances, Jimmy was just another ski bum like the rest of us. Of course, to those who knew him he was special, but in the broad scheme of things he was just another guy who lived for powder days and immediate gratification. That day though, Jimmy's life was relived in epic proportions. Stories of his qualities and transgressions were told with equal reverence—a reverence seldom bestowed on the living. After a person has passed their faults become eccentricities, misdeeds become colorful behavior.

As I watched the ashes scatter, I was reminded that the body is little more than a vessel on loan. Granted some vessels are better built and maintained; all will eventually decay. There is no amount of wealth, possessions or earthly accomplishments that can prevent the ultimate end. I was also reminded that monuments and memorials are wasted on those who did not know their inspiration. To be celebrated in death one must live a life of celebration—a life of taking chances, and making mistakes, friends and enemies.

With the job done, we pointed our skis off the summit. The bowl looked perfect with a foot of fresh and untouched. And the wind had stopped—a little gift from Jimmy. I couldn't help but notice that even those of us who climbed with difficulty looked strong and elegant while skiing down. I picked my line and jumped in. Twenty turns later, a coughing attack forced me to stop and take a breath. I pulled down my neck gaiter and found the inside covered with ashes. While we were spreading Jim's remains, some must have gotten on my clothing. When I zipped my jacket and pulled up my gaiter, a little of Jimmy's ashes got stuck in my throat choking me. Strange. I began skiing down again and the wind picked up. I swear I could hear him laughing…

CHAPTER 5: POLITICS

"Those who are too intelligent to engage in politics are punished by being governed by those who are not." –Plato.

I've always been interested in politics. I'm unabashedly liberal, biased, and recently elected. I'm not sure, but I might be the only Green Party elected official who has an unregistered handgun.

THE UGLY BACKSIDE OF POLITICS

Various Colorado Newspapers, *April 2004*

[Dateline: April 5, 2004, 10:30 p.m. on the night before municipal elections.]

A picture of my buttocks is circulating in cyberspace. This rather embarrassing situation is a result of my decision to run for public office.

If you haven't noticed, my column has been absent from the local paper and others. The editors felt that since I was running for office, my weekly column would be an unfair advantage for me over my competition. They were fearful that I would try to plant subliminal messages such as one recent effort published just before they laid me off.

The column in question read:

A lifetime of soap dishes and sugar bowls VOTE FOR ME were laid out and priced to sell. Ellen picked up a threadbare, wool blanket DON'T VOTE FOR THOSE OTHER GUYS and said, "This stuff is junk. No one will want this." I touched the worn wool with reverence and said, SEND ME MONEY "That was on my parents' bed."

Nine candidates were running for three seats on the town council. As I type this, the night of Election Day, I do not know if I captured one of the coveted seats or received fewer votes than Osama Bin Laden might. In truth, though I hope to win, I could also be very content with various configurations of the three council seats if filled by the many competent competitors.

My wife agreed that I could run for town council as long as my campaign costs didn't preclude me from paying all our bills and buying her skis. In the end, my total election expenses were less than what G.W. Bush's team has spent on gift-copies of the Koran.

Many of my fellow politicos were much more generous with their war chest dollars. They spent funds on media ads, t-shirts, yard signs and mass-mailings. One council wannabe even paid a young waitress to place a temporary tattoo bearing his campaign slogan on her thigh. I was angry over this display of poor taste, until my wife agreed to share the money she made for the service.

Overall, the campaign was positive and good-natured, but like anything else, one bad apple can spoil the bushel. It seems that some muckraking miscreant stole some of my rival's campaign signs and placed them in my garage; my staff is holding an investigation.

I've had a lot of fun running—with most of my enjoyment coming from the abuse I've been able to heap on my competitors, many of whom are close friends. In fact, my friendship with Rob is the reason my derrière is now spamming the World Wide Web.

When I learned that he had his own "Elect Rob" website, and after a few beers, I decided to e-mail his website a photocopy of my butt in protest.

I hasten to point out that no laws were broken. Yes, I might have been one beer over the limit, so I rode my bicycle to my buddy's office and photocopied my good side. Next, I rode to another friend's house, scanned the photo, and e-mailed it to myself (and, of course, I copied it to my wife). I returned home, logged on and was greeted with the words, "You've got mail."

Somewhere between taking the picture, scanning it and mailing it to myself, the image lost some of its appeal. But I already had a fair amount of time and beer invested in the project so I felt compelled to follow through.

Fortunately, my computer was smarter than me. Every time I tried to send the image to Rob's website, I received the error message that my backside contained a computer virus. Before I learned that my bottom was diseased, I had regrettably e-mailed it to a few friends and family members. The problem now is I've forgotten whom—I think this could be a liability if I choose to run for a higher office.

Tomorrow I'll know if my platform of legalized hemp products and homeland security struck a chord with the voters. As I mentioned before, my fellow candidates are all qualified and well intended. The beauty of politics at that local level is that with nothing much to gain, those who run do so for the best intentions; they simply want to give back to the place they love. It's a pity that that reality is missing in politics on a national level. I cannot imagine John Kerry sending a picture of his posterior to his rivals. Now Hillary Clinton, that's another story. I only wish I was on her mailing list...

~~~

LIBERTY AND JUSTICE FOR MOST OF US

Various Colorado Newspapers, *June 2002*

The skies were dark and quiet this July Fourth—a result of the ongoing drought, which has kept the skyrockets grounded. This was a refreshing change since it made for a period of quiet reflection and reminded me that you can still love something silently without lighting up the sky in a bombastic display of flash and sound.

I'm very grateful to be born in America. I'm particularly grateful to have been born, period. As I looked at the quiet skies on our country's birthday, some things bothered me.

I wondered, in a nation as wealthy as ours, why are there millions still who cannot afford health insurance or health care? I was curious why so many of our elderly are neglected and lonely. I was mad that a small Diet Coke and bag of popcorn at the local chain movie theater cost eight dollars. I wasn't happy with the fact that plastic surgeons make so much more income than teachers, nurses and paramedics. Why is Justin Timberlake a millionaire, while Muddy Waters died broke? A child can suffer with cancer as another season of television's Survivor airs. This makes me want to scream at the placid darkness.

One thing that did not bother me in the least (which seemingly puts me in the minority) was the ruling of the 9th U.S. Circuit Court of Appeals that mandatory recitation of the Pledge of Allegiance in public schools was in violation of the First Amendment.

It is understandable that the politicians would posture with a self-righteous indignation. Unlike universal health care and overpriced movie theater food, the Pledge of Allegiance was something our elected officials were actually willing to fight for. For the rest of us who work for a living, this is little more than an interesting lesson in the Court's quest at ascertaining our founding fathers' Constitutional intentions.

What I'm referring to here is the case of a California atheist with too much time on his hands, who filed suit to keep his daughter from being forced to pledge allegiance to God and the country in her public school. The court ruled in favor of the infidel, and then promptly put its decision on hold. I predict that when all is settled and resolved, little will have changed and, either way, it hardly matters.

It is of no great importance that the original Pledge of Allegiance was written by a Socialist, Baptist minister and included no mention of God or even the United States. Nor does it matter that The Daughters of the American Revolution and the Knights of Columbus, separated by thirty years, lobbied to have the words changed to suit their political and religious doctrines. What matters is that at this time in this country our energies would be better spent on real issues.

If merely reciting dogma caused children to become better citizens, perhaps the uproar is warranted. If that were the case, why not include a pledge never to smoke cigarettes, drive drunk and to always floss their teeth; while turning our children into patriots, we could also reduce lung cancer, highway deaths and dental discomfort. I'm not convinced most of the kids even know what they are saying. Until I was a senior in high school, I thought the words "Indivisible and justice for all" read "Invisible and just fall." I had no idea what I was saying.

We live in a great nation with great wonders and pride and, yes, great problems. I'm confident that someday, as the Pledge boasts, there truly will be liberty and justice for all. In the meantime, let's not get distracted by the noise and flash, but rather love our nation for its bounty and good intentions and realize there is still much to be done.

~~~

JACK RYAN COULD HAVE BEEN THE NEXT BILL CLINTON

Summit Daily News, July 2004

Illinois' fallen politician, Jack Ryan, could have been the golden child of the Republican Party. He has the looks of a young Ronald Reagan, the politics of a young Barry Goldwater and the wealth of an old Dick Cheney.

For those same reasons, he could have been the Democrat's worst nightmare.

Republicans like Ryan scare the Birkenstocks off of liberals like me. He is pro-family values, pro-guns and pro-Bush. And of course, he is anti-taxes, anti-freedom of choice and against same-sex unions. And to make matters worse, he is smart, personable and sincere.

He was raised in a large Irish Catholic family, graduated with honors from Dartmouth and Harvard and went to work for fifteen years at Goldman Sachs.

If those credentials weren't scary enough, Ryan turned his back on his lucrative career to help the poor. For the last three years, he taught at an all black, inner-city high school for a fraction of a fraction of his former salary. As far as I can tell, Jack Ryan practiced what he preached.

When he announced his intent to run for the U.S. Senate, endorsements came out of the woodwork. Conservatives like Jack Kemp and Bill Bennett lined up to welcome the Senate heir apparent into the ranks of the GOP. Ryan was hip, smart, handsome and devoted; some said he was a conservative version of Jack Kennedy.

Unfortunately for Ryan, and fortunately for us liberals, Jack Ryan had a bit of a skeleton in his closet—actually, it was an allegation of a skeleton.

Four years ago, when he was going through a contentious divorce, his wife made some kinky accusations.

To her credit, the ex-wife has refused to discuss the divorce. All she would say was that Jack Ryan is a good friend, a good man, and a loving father and was a faithful husband. The ex-wife went on to say that in her opinion, her former husband would make a wonderful senator.

Several media organizations sued for release of private court documents pertaining to the Ryan's divorce. A judge in California ruled that the public interest outweighed the concerns for privacy and the possible negative effect on the divorced couple's nine-year-old son.

Court records revealed that Ryan's wife had claimed that on three occasions he took her to a "bizarre sex club with cages, whips and apparatus hanging from the ceiling." It was at this club that he asked her to have sex with him while others watched.

Normally, this would be the time for me to gloat. Like many, I delight when the champions of family values are proven to be salacious. I love it when self-righteous public figures, the likes of Bob Barr, Strom Thurmond, Newt Gingrich, Jimmy Swaggert and Rush Limbaugh are discovered to be hypocrites.

In the case of Jack Ryan, I find myself gloat-less.

Under pressure from fellow Illinois conservatives, Ryan withdrew from the Senate race. The smart money opined that a conservative who preaches family values but then gets kinky at sex clubs is unelectable.

Even if the worse allegations were correct, Jack Ryan did nothing that could be called unfaithful, abusive or illegal.

He simply wanted to have sex with his wife while other adults watched. He wasn't even planning on charging admission. To be clear, his wife refused and they left the sex club.

Granted I'm a liberal, but I don't care about Jack Ryan's sex life. As long as what he does only involves adults and does not injure anyone, I don't think it matters.

Let's face it: some humans are sexually tweaked. All it takes is a walk down the dark side of the Internet to illustrate this point.

I feel sorry for Jack Ryan. Despite all he has achieved, all the good he has done, he will be remembered as the guy who wanted to make love to his wife in front of spectators.

While I don't care about Ryan's sex life, I *do* care about his politics. Much of what he believes in, I do not. But I also believe that he has often been totally sincere in regard to family values, homeland security and the right to bear arms. So what if he liked being spanked while wearing scuba gear.

Don't get me wrong; I'm glad he is gone. A Republican like him could be a formidable political foe. I only wish that he were drummed out of the campaign because of his beliefs, rather than his alleged sexual proclivities.

When our country becomes more concerned with the national debt and our propensity to wage war than with the sexual leanings and libidos of our leaders and citizens, we will be better served...

~~~

NOSE HAIR IN THE NAME OF HOMELAND SECURITY

Summit Daily News, August 2004

It was a disaster narrowly averted. This summer a middle-aged man was prevented from boarding a commercial airliner—he was armed with nose-hair clippers. I was that man.

I love knives. When I first met my mate, a vegetarian liberal from an intellectual family, she had trouble reconciling with herself that she was involved with a man who carried a shiv. I was unable to explain myself then, and I still can't. It might just be a force of habit left over from adolescence.

Not all my knives are dangerous. I have several small souvenir knives, some from childhood, with logos of Hopalong Cassidy, Niagara Falls, Boston Red Sox. I also love those small multi-tools with scissors, toothpicks, cranium drills and tweezers. There are various blades stashed in my briefcase, truck and daypack. Since 9/11, my wife insists I diligently perform a knife purge before we head to the airport. I always comply, not only to keep her happy but because I dread losing even one of my most inexpensive blades.

This summer I flew alone to my niece's wedding out in Boston. Before leaving home, I performed my preflight ritual. I left my handcrafted German stiletto on my desk. I removed a small multi-tool from my briefcase and took the small Swiss Army knife off my key chain.

Traffic at DIA was light. With only carry-on luggage I was able to arrive at security check-in early. To facilitate an easy passing I wore soft running shoes, a belt with a plastic buckle, and had removed the steel plate from my head.

With an air of superiority, I placed my bag on the scanning apparatus while others were asked to remove their shoes, belts and IUDs. As I took my garment bag from the conveyer belt, a uniformed lady grabbed it and said, "Will you come with me please?"

She placed my bag on a table between us and asked, "Do you have any weapons or metal objects in your bag?"

"I hope not," I responded honestly.

That evidently was the wrong answer since it brought another security person into the fray.

I sincerely thought it was a mistake. Not only had I left all knives behind but I also abandoned my small world band radio, money clip and metal Fischer Space Pen just to avoid an occurrence such as this.

After about ten minutes of searching, they found it. Tucked in the ripped lining of my shaving kit was an old pair of nose hair clippers, with a quarter inch blade—I thought I had lost them years ago. I should point out that I probably had flown several times with that same kit and scissors.

Both security personnel looked at me as if they had found a small child hogtied in my carry-on.

"You can't fly with this."

"I won't," I responded. And then I added, "I'm sorry, I didn't know it was in there."

I was then asked if I wanted to go back to ticketing to check-in my nose hair scissors, go to the post office and mail them to myself, or throw them away. I explained that the wedding was the next day and that if I was allowed to trim my nose hairs right then they probably wouldn't grow back before the reception.

I was told that federal law prohibits nose hairs trimming within one hundred feet of security. I opted for the throwaway option.

The other security guy lost interest and walked away. I was brought to a five-gallon bucket filled with tiny knives and scissors, and I tossed them in.

Before leaving, I apologized once again for taking up her time and explained that I didn't know the nose-weapon was in my shaving kit. But unable to help myself, I added, "I know that you are just doing your job, but don't you think taking nose-hair clippers from a fifty-year-old Irish guy is a little like getting your parakeet neutered because your cat got pregnant?" From her look, I knew I'd better get going.

Granted the world has changed since 9/11. I am willing to except a substantial loss of convenience and civil liberties in the name of homeland security. But it seems that what our government lacks in progress of adopting reforms to increase inter-departmental communication, tighten restrictions of cargo shipping and adopt the recommendations of the 9/11 commission, it makes up with picayune scrutiny of air travelers. With the current measures in place—sky marshals, reinforced cockpit doors—it is unlikely that terrorists will ever be able to hijack a plane with nose hair clippers.

There is the 'letter' of the law and the 'essence' of the reality. The letter of the law states that any cutting implement is a weapon. Reality affirms, the only ones who need to fear nose hair clippers are nose hairs…

~~~

PUTTING CASH WHERE YOUR BUMPER IS

Various Colorado Papers, *September 2003*

I've never walked away from a confrontation feeling better than I did before it began.

It was for that reason that I said nothing to the lady who'd cut me off only a few minutes earlier. It wasn't as if she threatened my life. She simply looked me in the eye, ran the stop sign and caused me to swerve and hit my brakes. Like most examples of aggressive driving, her effort did little good. We both ended up at the same place only minutes apart. When I pulled in next to her, she seemed to recognize my truck. She jumped out of her SUV and hurried away.

"Excuse me, ma'am," I said as I opened my door.

"What?" She spun on her heels, faced me; she was ready.

"You left your lights on," I said.

She relaxed only slightly and said, "They're on a timer. They'll shut off."

It could have been my imagination, but I noticed a sheepish look before she hurried away.

As I walked behind her vehicle, I looked back to see if her lights were really going to shut off. That's when I noticed her bumper sticker: "Commit random acts of kindness."

Bumper stickers represent how we would like to think of ourselves—a declaration of who we would like to be—but not necessarily how we are. In these polarized times, our bumper stickers are indicative of the strong feelings of the various camps. Part of me feels whatever it takes to get Americans politically and socially involved is a good thing. Unfortunately, bumper stickers are mere lip service to a cause and require little actual commitment. I'd like to change that.

I know you anti-government-intervention types will hit the roof on this, but I'm suggesting we create one more federal agency; Let's call it the office of Put Your Money Where Your Mouth Is.

This agency would be in charge of issuing bumper stickers. Citizens would go to one of many convenient locations and purchase the political slogans or Christian/Darwin fish emblems of their choice—the key word being "purchase."

Let's say you want to put a "We Support Our Troops" sticker on your Hummer. This agency would issue your bumper sticker only after you have pledged a substantial amount of money that would actually support our troops. Maybe for every million stickers sold, our government could buy a bomb or establish a fund to pay our soldiers' mortgages until they return home. By the same token those who chose to voice protest to the occupation of Iraq and Afghanistan could donate funds to Doctors without Borders, UNICEF and

Amnesty International. They'd then be issued a sticker that reads "Support Peace." Christian Fish stickers would only be given to those who can prove they tithe (donate ten-percent of wages) to a church and those who want to display the Darwin stickers must give to public education.

Of course, there would be no charge for those who wish to display allegiance for sport teams, college affiliations or product endorsements. Anyone willing to place a "Colorado Rockies" sticker on a vehicle should be encouraged. Moreover, "Grateful Dead" bumper stickers would be free because they let the cops know who to stop first at drug checkpoints.

When I was a kid, I wanted my old man to buy me a new bicycle; he agreed to pay for half. I mowed lawns to save for my share. On the way home from the store with my new bike in the trunk, my dad asked me to figure out how many hours of labor went into my purchase. We went over the hours we both worked for my new ride. His contention was that I should think of what I want in terms of how much I am willing to work to achieve it. He said, "If you're not willing to sacrifice for something, maybe you don't want it bad enough."

This program of paying for your agenda would go a long way in teaching the lesson that politics and policies are not free, nor do they come without human suffering and sacrifice. If you believe in war, you should be willing to fight or pay extra to have others do so. If you support peace, the least you can do is volunteer your time or give freely of your cash to organizations that promote your principals. Do I practice what I preach? Not always. I too am guilty of not always walking the walk of my ideologies. But that ends here and now. So in the spirit of exactitude, I'm removing my "Sexy Senior Citizen" bumper sticker from the fender of my Vespa motor scooter. Let no one accuse me of false advertising…

~~~

POLITICAL BATTLES WITH A BIG BROTHER

Summit Daily News, February 2004

The answering machine was blinking so I hit the button.

"Hey little buddy, this is your big brother, Mike. Sorry I missed you. I'm sure you're probably at a peace rally before heading to the welfare office. Is it true that you're picketing logging operations now that you've had your new home built? At any rate, my liberal little brother, you were missed over the President's Day weekend. The family said the pledge of allegiance and the Lord's Prayer in your honor. Despite your politics, we still love you."

My big brother Michael is a Republican. That said, he is a Republican with a sense of humor and is truly a compassionate conservative. He volunteers at least eight hours a week, walks the walk of Christianity and has raised three children to do the same. He recently became a legal guardian of a developmentally disabled middle-aged man, who was languishing in a state institution. When his three children left for college, he moved the man into his home.

Michael is a former Army intelligence officer, a devoted student of American history and more politically astute while sleeping than me on my best day. He believes in a small national government, local control of local issues, limited Federal and Supreme Court intervention and traditional values. He feels that this country should use its military might to promote peace and to overthrow despots around the world.

He also is one of the kindest men I've ever met, and with the exception of his wife's cooking I've never known him to lie about anything.

Whenever I need a conservative take on any issue I call my big brother, Mike. He has yet to sway me from my liberal leanings, but he is always good for a pervasive and logical argument from the opposing side of the aisle.

Mike has given me a peek into the other side of Roe vs. Wade, gun control, school prayer, welfare reform, tax relief and the invasion of Afghanistan and Iraq. He has tried to explain why sometimes commerce needs to take precedent over the environment and homeland security over civil liberties. He hasn't won me over, but he has shown me that my side does not have the market cornered on intellect and humanity.

When the Massachusetts Supreme Court issued a ruling that opened the door for same-sex unions, I called Mike to rub some salt in his wounds.

He was not at home at the time so I left him a message.

"Hey Stalin, this is your illegitimate little brother. I was very happy to hear that the courts in the motherland have ruled that couples of all sexual persuasions enjoy the rights and protection that marriage provides. Now you conservatives can finally get your eyes off the keyholes and your minds on your own business. That is, if you're not too busy rewriting the constitution to reaffirm your belief that God loves only you and shares your hatred of the Clintons and homosexuals."

Michael called back to tell me that he had just returned from church, where he had prayed for God's forgiveness of my past dalliances and current politics. He went on to take a couple of shots at Ted Kennedy and John Kerry. When he finally took a breath, I brought up the hundreds of same-sex couples who were lining up at courthouses across his state.

Michael shocked me by saying, "I walked by one courthouse on Friday. There must have been fifty of them on the sidewalk. It was beautiful."

I thought it was a trick so I cautiously waded ahead. "How can you say it was beautiful? These people are defying your Governor, President and Pope."

Mike said, "Sorry Comrade, I don't buy into that. It was beautiful because at that moment the street was filled with people who loved each other. You don't need to approve to feel that."

When I said his statement contradicted the position of his political party and church, he said, "Do I believe that God intended marriage as a union between a man and a woman? Yes. But I also believe that God intended the Red Sox to win the World Series, so I might be biased. If God has a problem with it, he can handle it himself. And as far as my President (Bush) and my Governor (Mitt Romeny) go, they should concentrate on uniting the country, rather than dividing us."

My brother then went on to add that he did not know any gay people—"Heck Little Brother, you're one of the few Democrats I talk to." He added that though he did not understand the gay lifestyle, he felt our government had better things to do than amending the Constitution to keep marriage heterosexual.

"Dang-it Biff, I wouldn't care if you decided to marry yourself. At least, you'd be finally having sex with the one person in the world who you find most attractive."

Alexis De Tocqueville once said, "In politics, shared hatreds are almost always the basis of friendships."

Honestly, what do the rest of us care if gays and lesbians want to get married and enjoy all the rights and misery that union provides?

My big brother Mike has taught me that it possible to be on the right and in the right at the same time...

~~~

BEATING THE BUSHES FOR A YOUNG REPUBLICAN

Denver Post, November 2002

"JOB OPPORTUNITY For an intelligent, engaging Republican woman. A sense of humor and excellent public speaking skills are essential. This is an entry-level position for a comely Conservative to gain a foot-hold in the exciting world of low-rent television. Short hours and shorter pay; NPR listeners need not apply."

Those words (more or less) appeared on help wanted cards placed on job boards around Summit County, Colorado. You'd think there would be a fair amount of interest from young Republicans, but that was not the case. The line of applicants was as short as a list of profitable businesses run by G.W. Bush. I know there are attractive and articulate conservative gals out there—Condoleeza Rice, Mary Matalin and Eva Braun to name a few. Since none of them were likely to work for ski-lift tickets, we still had a pair of jack-boots to fill.

I host a show called "Summit Speak Out." It airs on a small, gerbil-powered television station in the mountains. We like to think of ourselves as a high altitude "Meet the Press" with less funding and poorer grammar. I'm joined weekly by a cast of media types. Most of the panelists hover in the middle politically. I, on the flipside, carry pictures of Hillary Clinton and Che Guevara in my wallet.

In the past, my liberalism was offset on camera by the conservatism of a young female newspaper editor, who I suspected was secretly sensual, but could play the political prude. The young editor made her parents proud by marrying a sports reporter and moving to a community where the economy isn't gauged by annual snowfall.

Her leaving left a huge void on the panel. There is nothing worse than a pack of middle-aged, white bread, bleeding hearts pontificating on the good karma of social welfare without a balance of Grand Old Party lassie-fare capitalism. In keeping with the prevailing major network's policy of casting feminine charms as the foil of bloated male louts, our station felt we needed an attractive Republican, and we needed one fast.

Locating a young conservative in the hedonistic world of a ski resort is not an easy task. Not content to wait for them to come to us, I staked out book-burnings, church picnics and gun shows — to no avail.

The few applicants we did have were lacking either the political or on-camera requirements. One didn't even know who G. Gordon Liddy was. We finally settled for a retired Reagan-era State Department employee with an enlarged prostate and a goatee.

I guess I can't blame young people, especially single females, for not joining the GOP. If I were to define the two parties in philosophical terms, I'd say Republicans are angry and Democrats are sorry; Republicans are prudent and Democrats are horny. Now granted, this is coming from an admitted tax-and-spend liberal with a portrait of Trent Lott lining his hamster cage. That said, liberals not only dress better, but they seem to have more fun.

I think that is because liberals are more concerned with personal freedom and less with rules and morals. We don't tell woman what to do with their bodies, (okay, maybe Bill Clinton did but he always gave an Oval Office letter opener as compensation). And if you exclude Representative Trafficant, we have much better haircuts.

I'm sure there are plenty of charming, female conservatives who are well spoken and funny. There might even be a few in Summit County that we missed. Perhaps this column will ferret them out.

Unfortunately, I can't offer much in the way of compensation or working conditions. The studio is hot, the coffee is cold and most of the help have jailhouse tattoos. On the other hand, it could be an opportunity for a GOP gal to hang, albeit briefly, with the counter-culture. To sweeten the pot, I'd even throw in an old Charlton Heston video and some ski lessons (conservatives don't snowboard).

CHAPTER 6: CONNUBIAL BLISS

"Women need a reason to make love, men just need a place." I'm not sure who said that but I'd like to buy him a beer. Whether it lasts fifteen minutes or fifty years, love is the most divine aspect of the human condition. The sexes are certainly equal yet not at all alike. My mate is stronger,

*smarter and much more enlightened than me, yet I can still
make her cry and threaten to kill the rodents we catch in our
Have-a-Heart mousetraps.*

PORCELAIN ENVY, OR LOVE IN THE KITCHEN

Denver Post, February 2003

My wife asked if I was disappointed that we never make love standing up in the sink. She was concerned that the absence of washbasin-love was symptomatic of a marriage that lacked excitement. I was shocked by her question. Even as newlyweds, we never tested our sink's tensile strength. I had doubts it would handle our weight, and the garbage disposal feature frightened me.

Ellen's concerns stemmed from a book she was reading. It seems the heroes of this fiction are so consumed with passion that they make love any place they can get a decent foothold. Upon further interrogation, she also admitted they pass through mine fields, garrote ninja guards and assassinate Soviet double agents. I'm ashamed to say that Ellen and I don't do that stuff either.

I did my best to allay Ellen's fears and insecurities. The truth is, like most long-term couples, if we behaved now like we did when we first met, I'd have to quit my job and study yoga. Over the course of a long relationship, the excitement and novelty of discovery has been somewhat replaced by the comfort of trust and respect. After fifteen years together, though the sink is still used for cleaning, I could not be more content.

"The enemy of good is better."

I'm not sure who said that, but I could not agree more. So much of our time and energy is spent trying to make a good situation better that we don't appreciate what we already have. It wasn't too long ago that most people in this country were delighted to simply have a mate, a place to live and the means to support a family. Now to have only what you need is often not enough.

In our world, this bottomless desire is manifested in the obsession over our homes, our vehicles and our careers. But this can also be seen rearing its salacious head in marriages and relationships. There have been an inordinate amount of separations lately in my circle of friends. Many claim irreconcilable differences. I have a newsflash for anyone considering marriage: Your mate will never be perfectly compliant to your needs and wishes; if she were, you'd have to pay her. After watching friends swap spouses like leased vehicles, I've come to the conclusion that the relationship grass is seldom greener — it just has a better sprinkler system.

When I see an elderly couple sitting together and holding hands like young lovers, I often wonder what fanned the flames of their union. Was it the hot fire of passion or the slow burn of respect and friendship? I would guess a little of both. But I would also suggest they share an unconditional love and have long accepted each other's peculiarities and faults.

In my town, there is a fundraiser called the "Parade of Homes." Walking through the splendor of these houses, you assume that residing in such opulence would ensure happiness. When I've taken the tour, I never got a warm feeling. I'd wager that the novelty of comfort for the residents has long ago worn off. If you want to see a joyful house, find one where a young couple has saved and sacrificed and can now finally afford. There should be a fundraiser called "Parade of Crude Cabins."

A good relationship goes deeper than a huge home or sexual athletics. I won't deny that I'd love to live in one of those mountain mansions with big rooms, indoor pools, and a bidet in the garage, but only if my bride came with the package. Our lives are never perfect, nor are those who you share it with. But if you take the time to take stock in your blessings you'll usually find that you have it pretty good. I don't take my gifts for granted. I have my health, most of my teeth, some of my hair and a woman who thinks I'm funny. And next week the plumber arrives to put a handrail around the sink…

~~~

FROM THE FIRST DANCE TO THE LAST BOMB

Summit Daily News, July 2004

As the bride and groom danced for the first time as man and wife, it dawned on me that whether it lasts for fifty years or only fifteen minutes, love is the most wonderful aspect of the human existence.

Don't look for any underlying message in this story. Greater minds than mine have dedicated volumes to the subject of love with only mixed success. But watching that slow dance made me want to at least take a stab at it.

Though love is fun with a partner, it also makes a wonderful spectator sport. For that, there is no better venue then a wedding. Watching the newlyweds whisper and touch hands; seeing the pride and hope in the faces of their parents; raising a glass as the best man struggles to keep his composure as he toasts a brother he adores and respects. It would have choked me up even if there weren't an open bar.

This is the summer for weddings for my mate and me. Between May and October, we will have attended four or five. Though each couple and family will be different, the celebrations will be much the same. We will all come together to rejoice in the commitment and hope for the best. Jews will marry gentiles, Irish will wed agnostics and some old guys will walk away from the altar with a new young wife. What they all will have in common is from that first dance on all things are possible.

It has always been my contention that just because a smart guy says something doesn't make it true. But this is one expression that broaches little debate: "Love conquers all." A lesser-known second phrase of that quote by Virgil: "Let us surrender to love."

I'm guessing that half of all marriages didn't end in divorce in Virgil's time, so perhaps he was waxing a little optimistic. Maybe if he were around today, he'd amend it to, "Love conquers all...for a while." The last thing on anyone's mind at the bar or the buffet is the possibility of the relationship not enduring.

As a teenager, I laughed at that song by John Lennon, "All You Need is Love." I thought it sentimental and trite. It was my teenaged opinion that love was pretty nice, especially if you got some from Peggy O'Malley, but there were more important things in the world—like having an older brother who would buy you Playboy magazines. I've since outgrown that belief.

Whether it is the passion and promise of a couple in love, the unconditional devotion of a parent and child, or the basic understanding and acceptance of human diversity, John Lennon's words ring with a simplistic truth. Call it unsophisticated, naïve, or the ravings of a sixties burnout, but in my opinion, what this country needs now more than anything is love and compassion.

It seems that just as individuals differ in their capacity to show kindness and humanity so do nations and cultures. This country is suffering from a serious lack-of-love dry spell (a condition that many mountain males are quite familiar with).

Perhaps it is because I'm at the age where I'm finally paying attention, but since the sixties I've never seen this nation so polarized. We cannot debate without name-calling. We don't disagree over philosophies as much as we denounce the morals and intellect of our challengers. Like a bull in a china shop, we have reduced the rest of the world into either for us or against us categories.

Some might argue that 9/11 changed the world. The spread of mistrustful suspicion and rejection of human kinship has been almost as tragic as the lives we lost.

I see little compassion in our government's policies and practices. It seems we waste too much energy propagating an us vs. them agenda, both nationally and abroad. This heavy-handed foreign policy has done little but exacerbate the dangerous global situation.

The world is unsettled and unsafe. Old hatreds exceed our collective memory and continue to fester. With so little in shared religion, history and values, the search for any common ground can seem daunting. But as Virgil and Lennon would attest, there are some basic creature needs, desires and truths. Declarations like "love conquers all", "all you need is love" and "don't pee on electric fences" (the last one is mine) are cross-cultural certainties. Though so much separates the various creeds and cultures, we have a fair amount in common: the desire to protect our lands, to love our families, and to enjoy the pleasure of watching newly-weds dance. And of course, the joy of an open bar…

~~~

CHOPPING DOWN THE KINDRED TREE

Vail Daily News, August 2001

Some would describe my family as dysfunctional; some would be correct. When certain members of my clan shop for a new refrigerator, they'll ask the sales clerk if there is room enough inside to store human heads. Among the six of us, we've been through divorce, addiction, intervention, rehab, psychotherapy and one even joined the Republican Party. Nevertheless, I can honestly say that among my family are some of the most intelligent, funniest and kindest people I've ever met.

Despite of, or perhaps because of my relation's peculiarities, I married into the Walton family. My bride's background is one of Norman Rockwell normalcy, coma-like calmness and perfect teeth.

You might think that such a white bread group would not welcome my family into their homes. But from the onset, her folks and family were excepting and nonjudgmental. Many parents would have resented their youngest child keeping company with a convicted miscreant over a decade her senior with limited means of support. They received and honored my weird family and me into their hearts and homes. They never questioned when my brother showed up at our wedding rehearsal dinner wearing a thong and a top hat, or why the monogrammed towels I gave them for Christmas had the wrong initials. While my family could be described as deranged yet festive, Ellen's is balanced, benevolent and yes, a little boring.

So when we traveled to northern Minnesota to attend my bride's family reunion, I didn't expect much excitement. Ellen's clan migrated to the Midwest—the land of the chosen frozen—from Scandinavia in the early 1900s.

When her forefathers partied, they partied hardy. There are sidesplitting stories of her grandfather, Sweden, who in a fit of craziness, would plow his fields with his shirt on backwards. And if that isn't wild enough, the tales still fly about her wacky uncle Hanz with his crazy collection of bowling shirts. Nourished by a diet of hard work and lutefisk, the family flourished. At our particular gathering, there were five generations—most with blonde hair and blue eyes. Though Ellen's immediate family was obviously the gentrified part of the cult, the rest were fine examples of Middle America. The two matriarchal sisters, named Anna and Dotty, were farm-raised and clear complexioned. They were round, stoic, and both were closing in on one hundred. The youngest in attendance was a three-year-old towhead named Carl. He ran around the gathering like a cat in a thunderstorm, punctuating his open field sprints with violent screams. Carl seemed a prime candidate for Ritalin, but his mother insisted he was a gifted child. (Is it my imagination, or are there more gifted children now than twenty years ago?)

The weekend began with a reception and cocktail party for fifty people. The mood and posture of the event was one of a junior high dance. The men stood on one side, hands in pockets, uncomfortable in their new clothing, arguing over fishing bait. Across the room the woman gathered in clusters, discussing their gifted children. If any gathering needed alcohol, it was this one. When Ellen's uncle, Boots, asked if I wanted to split a beer, I thought he was joking, but he was not. Before long, most of the group were divvying up cans of cold ones and discussing the recently finished ice-fishing season. For me, this was a pleasant and relaxing change from my Boston Irish experience of drinking, singing and fighting at family functions. Though I had little in common with Ellen's relatives, they were good, if not benign, company.

Following the reception, there was a boat ride, then a cookout and a tractor pull. It was midway through a horseshoe tournament that I began to notice some of them seemed to have difficulty pronouncing vowels. By the time dinner was over, many were openly fighting for the last can of Hams Beer and rehashing the distribution of their grandparents' estates. Before long, fights were breaking out over vintage Nash Ramblers, ice shanties and lawn tractors.

I worked the crowd and made small talk. Being a student of family neurosis, I made it my business to learn as much ancestry drama as possible. What I found was that when it came to dysfunction, even the wholesome are not exempt. Among this crowd of clear skin and clean living were assorted stories of dirty divorces, financial philandering and abused snowmobiles. That weekend made me feel better about my own heritage. I've come to the conclusion that all bloodlines host a combination of love and dysfunction. You might need to look deep to find the dysfunction and then a little deeper to see the love, but it is all there. Love and affection seems to flow more freely to those of like-lineage.

You can pick your friends, but you inherit your family. Or like my uncle-in-law Boots is fond of saying, "I'd rather spend time with this gang than have a fish hook in my lip."

~~~

SHARE THE LOVE, SHARE THE PAIN

Summit Daily News, May 2003

"Don't you dare break your leg and ruin my summer."

As soon as my mate issued the ultimatum, she realized she was in trouble. That is the downside of being married to someone like me who makes a living by telling only his side of a story.

It was late May in the San Juan Mountains near Silverton, Colorado. We were on a hike with our dog when the trail crossed a twenty-foot-wide creek, full of raging spring runoff that splashed over large pointed rocks. Even with a rope, there was no way we could have crossed safely. We followed the shore upstream for almost a mile, looking for a protected place to ford the creek. Eventually, we came to a spot where a rusted pipe (a relic from the mining era) spanned the river about five feet above the rocks and boiling water.

The pipe was fairly wide and looked old, but it seemed sturdy. I picked up my twenty-pound terrier and began to shuffle across the cylinder. If I felt like my bridge was going to collapse, I would try to heave my dog and myself to the far shore. Despite my well-thought-out plan, I was still a little nervous.

My dog smelled my fear. For once, he didn't whine, fidget or cry while being carried. He remained as quiet and still as a stuffed animal. When I reached the half-way point, I knew that the mining artifact was going to hold my weight. We were only five or six feet from the safety of the opposite shore when my mate, unable to stand the tension, exclaimed, "Don't you dare break your leg, and ruin my summer."

As soon as those words came out of her mouth, she knew it was a statement with some shelf life. In other words, I'd be telling the story for years to come. She looked chagrined and I began to laugh. Robby, sensing that the danger had passed, wet himself.

Ellen followed us across the pipe over the river. The first thing she said to me as she reached the far shore was, "You can't tell anyone I said that."

I said, "Don't worry, I won't."

If you take my mate's statement out of context, you'd think she was a hard-hearted woman. But in truth, Ellen's exclamation was both honest and under-standable. It also illustrates another advantage of a healthy long-term relationship: for better or for worse, you're in it together.

The "better" part is easy. You simply enjoy your successes and good days. But in truth, though sharing the bliss is pleasant when things are good, it's also easy to go it alone. When the "worse" rears its ugly head, a loving partner is worth her weight in Irish whiskey.

There's no doubt if I fell and broke my leg, or worse, my mate would nurse me through my ordeal. A significant other is your companion, mate and lover, but she is also a second opinion and a conscience to remind you when you are about to do something foolish. Ellen sees my talents and weaknesses clearly and is forced to live with the repercussions of my overconfidence. It is my habit to assume I'm graceful and bulletproof; it's her job to remind me that I'm not.

Forty years ago, when my father used to head out on a Sunday afternoon on my brother's motorcycle with me on the back and a flask in his pocket, my mother would yell to him as we left our driveway. "If you break your damn-fool neck, I'll bury you in your work clothes so I can give your good suit to my next husband." She would then add, "And remember you have your youngest son on the back so be careful."

It didn't dawn on me that if my father broke his damn-fool neck with me on the back, it might not bode well for my own damn-fool neck.

In truth, had my old man gotten hurt, my mother would have been overwhelmed, both emotionally and financially. Hers was a generation where the husband made the money and the wife raised the children (in her case, six). If something prevented my father from bringing home a paycheck, it would have caused dire financial straights for our family.

It's different for my mate and me. With no kids and little obligations, if one of us were to be incapacitated due to injury or deadness, we'd be devastated, but no meals would be missed.

The pain endured by one's spouse is shared by the other. Just last week, Ellen came home scraped up pretty badly from a mountain bike crash. I saw her limping toward the house from the second floor window. I ran down the stairs to comfort her, dress her wounds and to be sure she didn't get blood on our freshly shampooed carpets. Love is blind, but not necessarily stain resistant...

~~~

A HOUSE WITH MANY DIFFERENT COLORS

Vail Daily News, January 2003

My wife sat up in bed at 3:30 a.m. screaming the words "plum blossom."

I must say I was startled. Plum Blossom has never been her pet-nickname for me so I could only deduce that she was screaming someone else's name. I might have let it slide and gone back to sleep, but when she piped up she elbowed me in the face. "Damnit, Ellie," I said. "I think you broke my nose, and who the hell is Plum Blossom?"

My fear was that Plum Blossom might be the tattooed sushi chef who served us the night before.

When I confronted her with my suspicion, she looked at me as if I were crazy.

"I want plum blossom in our bedroom," she said. "And I barely touched you. Go back to sleep...after you get me a glass of water."

I was about to tell her that if she thought I was going to engage in a ménage à trois with some young buck, smelling of raw fish and named after a flowering tree, she could think again.

Then it dawned on me—she was just anguishing over what colors to pick for our hopefully, soon-to-be completed house.

Sometime this decade, we will finally move into our new house. Part and parcel with the price was a plain and boring white interior paint job. My bride's parents thought they were doing us a favor by footing the bill for a custom color job. Instead, they opened a Pandora's Box of indigo indecision.

My mate is brilliant, beautiful, strong and graceful as a gazelle, but with the home decorating skills of a tractor. If you leave out the strong, pretty, smart and graceful aspects, I'm the same way. Since neither of us quite have the interior design talent of Martha Stewart's pit bull, we were at a loss to choose a color scheme.

Lucky for us, our house is being erected in part by the contractors of Ice, Plumbing and Heating, whose motto is, "Moving at glacier speed to build you a better abode."

That being the case, we've had ample time to come up with enough wall-covering options to cause our painter to consider another occupation.

I've found the best way to maintain a healthy marriage is to let my spouse think she is getting her way. It's been my experience that this is best accomplished by always yielding to her way. For that reason, I've stayed out of the color-choosing game. I also felt it was best if the house painter hated only one of us.

If the Bush administration had an ounce of sense, it would deregulate marijuana and regulate Sherwin Williams. What kind of sadistic, polychromatic maniac comes up with all those colors and names?

For the last six months, I've been tripping on color charts and rolling over them in bed. If I stared at those samples until hell froze over, I would not be able to tell the difference between dragon fruit, feverish, or impatient pink (just three of the 24 designations of pink offered in the catalog).

Once finished, our love nest will be capable of sexually exciting a hummingbird. Our living room is laudable lime. Plum dandy surrounds both toilets. The kitchen is covered by ice plant, and when and if we throw in plum blossom in the bedroom, the place will look like a school of tropical fish. I'm a little worried about hallucinogenic flashbacks.

I got Ellen a glass of water. She took a sip and I waited for her to calm down. "Ellie, I thought we agreed on obstinate orange for the bedroom. That was after you had Dan the painter cover over that wall you had him paint with peach fuzz pink." If we tell him you now want plum blossom, he'll walk off the job."

I gave her a Tylenol PM to put her out for the rest of the night. Just as she was dropping off to sleep she mumbled the word, "kumquat." "Kumquat," I said. "What wall in the house do you want painted kumquat?"

Ellen sat up in bed and looked at me like I was crazy. "I don't want any wall painted kumquat," she said with disgust. "That's the name of the sushi chef with all those cute tattoos."

~~~

LOVE, BARGAINING AND A SOILED PET

Summit Daily News, June 2003

Robby came home with a "bad butt." I should point out that Robby is a twenty-pound terrier.

Without being too explicit, a bad butt is brought about by an irritated digestive tract, caused by eating trash, combined with the excessively hairy bottom of a dog. The result is often called "dingle berries," "soiled seat" or "dirty dumper."

Ellen and I love our pet. He is the child we'll never have—we hope. We like to cuddle and wrestle, and we allow him on the furniture. But as you can imagine, there is little pleasure had in rolling on the living room floor with such an encrusted hound.

My wife was the first to notice Robby's condition. She had returned from a run; I was working in my office. When I heard her scream, "God, that is so disgusting," I assumed she had found the long underwear I had hung in the refrigerator to dry. She came into the room with a look of horror and said, "Robby has a big-time bad butt, and you have to clean it."

My wife and I have a precise and well-defined division of labor in regards to household chores and obligations. I clean, dust, do the dishes and care for the cur—she doesn't. But when it comes to the family pet with a bad butt, all bets are off. So I turned to my mate and asked, "If I clean Robby, what will you do for me?" As an astute negotiator Ellen did not open with her best offer.

"If you clean the dog, I'll flush the toilet."

I told her that she would have to do considerably better than that. I was bargaining from a position of strength. Ellen, for all her stamina and earthiness, is finicky when it comes to disgusting things and odious objects. I, as a member of the media, am a hard man to gross-out.

It took several minutes, but we were able to reach an agreement. Ellen would cook dinner, do the dishes, remove her dirty bike shorts from the doorknob, and flush the toilet; I'd clean the dog.

My side of the bargain was much like a Republican's honeymoon—unpleasant and mercifully short. Ellen's was just the opposite. Thus, I was able to meet my obligations and get back to work while my mate's commitment was barely half completed.

Before too long, we sat down to a meal of Ellen's famous bean, broccoli and butter burritos while a freshly laundered dog frolicked on the floor. After dinner, Ellen began the clean up while I sat back and enjoyed her equally famous dessert specialty of beans, broccoli and butter tarts. I think both of us were happy with the deal we had struck. I think the key to a happy union is negotiation.

In our parent's generation, the roles of the sexes were defined. My mother cooked, cleaned, raised the children and ran the house. My father worked, scared the kids and worked some more. Now in this country, excluding Utah, the sexes are equal. The traditional roles have blurred with both partners sharing the responsibilities of livelihood and domestic obligations. In our household for example, while Ellen might not bring home quite as much bacon as I do, she is not afraid to chip in and help eat the BLTs.

In truth, relationships, or life for that matter, are often inequitable. That is where love, the great equalizer, comes in. I'm of the opinion that most love is conditional. You love someone for their spirit, soul and how they make you feel. You also love someone because they love and put up with you. It is often a mere matter of quid pro quo. "I'll love you despite your anal peculiarities and obsession with feather dusters and latex, if you'll love me even though I'm messy around the house and work less than Latoya Jackson." But through it all you must communicate and negotiate.

The house was clean, the dishes done. It was time to hit the sack. I took Robby out for one last sniff before bedtime. He was completing his nighttime ritual of marking his turf and growling at moths. We were about to head back when our neighbor Kim approached. She and I exchanged pleasantries for a minute and I was about to say goodnight when she said, "I'm sorry about the mess I made of your dog." I asked for a clarification and she said that her four-year-old had dropped his chocolate fudge ice cream on the sidewalk in front of our house.

"Robby immediately pounced on it," she said. "I didn't want him to get sick so I grabbed him by his collar. Luckily, he didn't get a chance to eat much, but when I hauled him up by the collar I caused him to sit on the melted ice cream.

I walked inside to find Ellie putting the dishes away. "I heard you through the window talking to Kim. What did she have to say?"

"Not much," I answered...

~~~

THE COLD REALITY OF A CHILLY MATE

Backcountry Magazine, January 2004

My wife is frigid and, of course, she blames me.

This is a fairly recent phenomenon. Six months ago, "frigid" was the last word that could be used to describe her. Unfortunately much is not the same since then. First, what was once a comfortable Indian summer has turned into a butt-cold winter. That alone is not the culprit in my mate's frostiness. She's lived in the high country for too many ski seasons to be chilled by an ambient temperature of twenty-below-zero. If I were to cast blame, it would have to be a two-pronged accusation of the rising cost of heating our home and my own cheapness.

According to reports, the price of natural gas has increased by as much as seventy-five percent. You might think this would also be reflected in the price of Mexican food, but that's not the case. Since we heat our home with gas and have witnessed that cost almost double, I've been on a campaign of conservation.

My fiscal philosophy for life in a ski resort town is nothing ground breaking. It is simply the art of balancing how much money I earn with how much I spend. My past money saving programs have included drinking powdered milk, biking and walking rather than driving, and trying to use both sides of the toilet paper. My wife hates dry milk, drives to the bathroom, and won't even discuss my TP suggestions. When it came down to setting our thermostat, she was less than willing to compromise. Finally, after much pleading on my part, she granted a meeting to negotiate.

Both of us agreed that a household temperature of sixty-eight-degrees-Fahrenheit was comfortable. From there we offered our various suggestions of a setting we could live with. I said fifty; she countered with sixty-five. For the first time in our marriage, I won. We set the heat to fifty-five.

The compromise has had many advantages and only a few drawbacks. Though the rate increase would normally double our bills, we now pay about thirty percent more than this time last year. By the same token, our electric usage (mostly by the refrigerator) has gone way down. We now put items in the fridge to warm them up. Food left out on our counters doesn't spoil, and houseguests seldom stay more than one night.

The only drawback I should mention is that cold temps will drain romance out of a home like a pair of two-year-old twins with colic. To combat this, I bought a space heater and strategically placed it in the bedroom. When love is in the air, I turn on the breeder-heater to pre-heat the boudoir. Now this is something that Public Service will not tell you: you only need to heat the room in which you're likely to find love-congress; save the garage for summer use.

My mate has been putting up with my program of conservation begrudgingly. We turn down the heat when we know we'll be gone the entire day skiing and when we go to sleep at night. One problem we've encountered is the shock of climbing between sheets that are as cold as a gas-meter-reader's heart. We looked into an electric blanket to toast our bed before turning in, but we were told that studies have linked electric blanket use to brain tumors. Until I can research the comparable cost of treating a tumor to the price of utilities, we're holding off.

There is very little the consumer can do to protest. We all must simply deal and wait for the rates to decrease. The big questions left are why, how and when.

Why has the cost of heating our homes risen so high? How will all those who can't afford this rate hike cope with a cold winter? When is this pattern likely to change?

The answers are as diverse as the political leanings of my friends. My liberal friends blame gas companies for their greed. My conservative friends (one of them works in the natural gas industry) blames my liberal friends for their hypocrisy of demanding cheap energy while, in the name of the environment, making it difficult for the energy producers to produce.

I'm not sure whom I believe. What I do know for sure is that with this huge increase the rich can afford it, the poor must endure it, and those of us in the middle must do the best we can. That being the case, I think I'll end it here. I just heard the breeder-heater fire up—duty calls…

CHAPTER 7: GOD

Whose name does God scream during sex? That all depends, but I believe in a divine power and have faith that she has a sense of humor. 'Cause if she were screaming my name, she'd have to.

PLAYING GOD IN A PINE TREE

Various Colorado Newspapers, *September 2000*

Gary Black thought I was God, literally.

It was a thoughtless prank played on a simple intellect, but the feeling of power it gave me was obscene.

Gary and his mother lived just behind my family's home on Boston's south shore. In the parlance of the times, Gary would have been described as retarded. He was also sweet, tender and gullible. I took advantage of that innocence. He believed I was God, and I let him.

It was the day John F. Kennedy was killed. Our class was called to the assembly hall. Our crying principal told us that our president had been murdered. Though miles and money separated Kennedy's world from the rest of the city, to those of us from the Boston area, JFK was ours—he was our hero and fueled our faith. We were sent home from school to mourn, reflect and bother our parents. My two best friends, Clete and Keith, and I decided to grieve the loss of our president and celebrate his life, by hiding in the "Big Tree" smoking cigarettes stolen from my mother's purse.

The Big Tree was a huge pine located in a vacant lot. It was the largest tree in our neighborhood. The top of the Big Tree was blown off in an ancient storm leaving a relatively flat platform, a perfect place for a tree house. My friends and I erected a simple structure among the thick boughs with free wood from a local construction site. In retrospect, I guess the wood wasn't meant to be free, but when we went to get it at night, no one was there to say otherwise.

Our tree fort was posh. It had a floor, a few walls, a bucket of rocks (for defense), milk crates to hold our stash of cigarettes and some girly magazines. In today's terms, it would be called affordable housing.

Our sanctum was impossible to see from the ground, and the exclusive property of Keith, Clete and me. "Death be to those who trespass" was inscribed on the sign nailed to the entrance. Those attempting to climb the tree could expect a rock shower.

It was a beautiful fall day—one of the last nice ones before winter. We squatted on milk crates, smoked, spit and talked tough. We speculated whether the Commies had killed our president, and if America would require the services of three kids to go undercover to seek retribution against the Red Menace. We loaded our BB guns, sharpened our jackknives and vowed revenge. I didn't allow myself to cry until after my friends went home.

As luck would have it, Gary Black was passing under the tree as I issued an audible sob over the death of our president. Another passerby might have deduced that someone was up in the tree, but Gary just assumed the cries came from the heavens.

He asked with a concerned naiveté, "Why are you crying, God?"

Gary thought I was God; I played along. I sucked back my sobs, composed myself and said in a deep voice.

"Well Gary, I'm crying because John F. Kennedy was killed."

Gary thought about that for a while and said, "He was good wasn't he, God?"

I answered that JFK was indeed good.

"Then, don't cry," Gary added. "He'll be in heaven with you soon."

Obviously, since this occurred almost forty years ago my memory is blurred. I've told the story so many times that the facts and the fiction, which make for a good story, tend to merge. But one thing that is independent of fact or fiction is that Gary talked to God and God talked back. What a rush.

To this day, I'm not sure if my behavior was a cruel gesture or a gift. Granted, it was wrong to impersonate a divine entity, but on the other hand it was all the same to Gary. He probably was and still is of the mind that he had a conversation with his God. Divinity was taken out from the books, stories and Sunday school and replaced with a physical, audible manifestation. I wish I could be so lucky.

Although I'm theologically confused, I wholeheartedly believe in a divine entity. I have no idea if God has any affiliation with the countless organized religions alive today. My guess would be that He has a small part in all faiths. I also hope and pray God has a sense of humor when it comes to young boys impersonating Him. If He is ticked off, he hasn't mentioned it to me. I've asked.

Because when I'm not masquerading as the Lord, I talk to him. Some might call it prayer, but my dialog isn't confined to God's ear. I talk to my departed mother, to friends, to relatives and to Booger (our long dead family pet). Every time someone I love passes away, I hope for contact. When I'm alone and in a beautiful place in nature, I'll ask for a sign: voices, trumpets, a burning bush, a sniffed crotch (Booger loved to do that) — I'd take anything.

Some would argue that the beauty of nature is a godly sign. Sorry, that's not good enough. I want trumpets.

Simplicity lends itself to trust; in that respect, Gary was lucky. He spoke to his God and received a response. If the voice and speech impediment sounded familiar to him, he made no mention of it. Maybe one sign that there is a payback of divine blessings is that to the gentle, kind and uncomplicated like Gary, faith comes easily…

~~~

CANS, BOTTLES AND THE WORD OF GOD

Various Colorado Newspapers, *January 2002*

"Can I give you my personal testimony of a life blessed by the Holy Spirit and my awakening to my Lord Savior?"

I didn't want to appear rude. The young man standing at my door took the time to put on a necktie and climb up two flights of stairs. But on the other hand, I was just heading out to Christmas shop and recycle my wife's whisky bottles, and time during the holiday season is a precious commodity.

I truly had too much to do and too little time to do it, but it was almost Christmas—a time for patience and giving. I was caught between a desire to be kind and a need to get busy, when a win-win solution dawned on me.

"May I give you my testimony?" he asked again.

"Sure," I said. "If I can give you my recycling."

The deal was made. I would give the young man my undivided attention. In turn, he would take my bottles and cans. I even offered to call some neighbors who might be interested in a similar deal. With one trip to the recycling center, he might be able to give several testimonies.

His story was sincere, though benign. He was raised middle class in the Midwest. An average student, he had little interest in the things that absorbed most kids. He wasn't unhappy, just indifferent. He went to a community college where he got involved with a Bible study group because a young lady who he had a crush on asked him. Once Jesus came into his life he was a changed person. He no longer lacked direction, or felt indifference. He had a mission and a purpose. So while the rest of his family was skiing on their Christmas vacation, he would take half the day to go door to door seeking converts.

After he told his story, he gave me some pamphlets containing scriptures. I was tempted to tell him that eventually those too would need to be recycled. He asked me what the depth of my relationship with God was? He asked me if I ever felt lost or tempted? He said that during these troubling times, we all needed the Lord in our lives. I was polite and respectful. I figured the young man had earned my attention, but it was time to go.

I asked him if he would like to take an energy bar to eat later. He graciously accepted. I handed him one and walked him down to the stairs to the parking lot. We came close to parting as friends when he turned to me and said, "The Godless in America must bear some of the responsibility for the recent terrorist attacks and suffering."

I felt like hitting him.

Instead, I told him that in my opinion there is a thin line between the self-righteous and the self-righteously violent. I reminded him that the antagonists in the 9/11 tragedy believed that they were following the edicts of the Almighty. I told him that historically, no God, be it Christian, Muslim or Judaic, is guiltless in terms of evil committed in their name. I told him that he should serve his God, revel in his faith and love all people. But I cautioned him not to feel superior or anointed to a degree where he considers himself ordained to make judgments or cast blame. That's when he tried to give me my recycling back.

After I calmed him down and placed my cans and bottles in the back seat of his rental car, he backed out of his parking space. Before he pulled away, he rolled down his window and said, "There is no gray, when it comes to the word of God, only black and white. You are either in his graces or not."

Not wanting to prolong the argument and risk having to do my own recycling, yet unable and unwilling to allow him the last word, I said, "I love you."

He looked at me closely, as if trying to gauge my sincerity. Satisfied, he said, "God Bless." Then he drove away.

As I watched him head off, I remembered what my old man used to say. "Never talk politics with friends or religion with strangers." By definition, faith and politics are comprised, in a large part, of opinions. I think it is encouraging when others live the life of their beliefs. Personally, I just can't seem to totally buy into one belief or party at the exclusion of all others. I do know that love, forgiveness and generosity are the prevailing tenets of all faiths. And I also know that any evil or unkindness committed in the name of any God is only the bastardized distortion of zealots. And with complete faith and conviction I can say that taking the time to hear the story of a stranger's journey is a small price to pay for the luxury of not having to recycle.

~~~

I SAW GOD...I THINK

Backcountry Magazine, November 2003

I knew the guy sitting under the bristlecone pine tree wasn't God. He couldn't be. For one thing, he was wearing snowshoes (most theologians agree that the Almighty telemarks). For another, he reeked of marijuana. In his defense, he didn't actually say he was the Almighty, but he did take credit for God's good work.

I was ski touring with my dog up a popular back-country trail at twilight on the day I encountered him. The sky just above the horizon was full of the wispy remnants of clouds after a light snow and gave off an eerie pink hue. The two inches of fresh snow did little to lesson the grip or glide of my light waxable skis. The wind was still and the air held a cold crispness that was an enticement to keep moving. It might have been the stark beauty, or perhaps the anti-inflammatories, but my body actually felt good as I climbed the slight incline. About halfway to the summit the trail contoured and wound around a small drainage complete with a frozen creek, several fir trees and a lone bristlecone pine. The recent snow had coated the branches casting a near supernatural silhouette against the blood-red sky.

Stopping to rest, I found myself surrounded by impossible beauty. Often the difference between your average run-of-the-mill exquisite setting and a profound aesthetic moment is the ability to appreciate your surroundings completely unhindered. Perhaps it was the beauty, or maybe it was the fact that my in-laws had finally left after a weeklong visit–but at that moment I was well aware of and very thankful for all my blessings.

"Thank you, God!" I bellowed.

The wind chilled my sweat; my dog peed on a low hanging branch and seemingly out of nowhere came the words, "You're welcome."

As a child, before I became a card carrying Catholic, replete with the comfort and guilt that only that faith can supply, I had to memorize a litany of prayers. A certain amount was required before I received my First Communion and many more before I made my Confirmation. Although I let my Papal club membership expire and no longer regularly attend mass, I still can recite those godly supplications: The Lord's Prayer, Act of Faith, Act of Contrition, Hail Mary, Glory Be. All of these can be dredged up from the depths of my brainpan. Mostly, I'm content to leave them there and stick with my own praying habits. If I'm going to talk to God, why plagiarize someone else's words?

Usually my prayers come in the form of simple requests or expressions of gratitude and are directed to any god who will listen. I'm not choosy in regards to the divine entity that answers my prayers. Whatever omnipotent being is up at bat at any given time is more than welcome to hear my thanks or requests. I'm certain the Jewish God has saved my hair, a Catholic one has kept me employed, a Muslim deity protects my knee cartilage and ligaments and a Haitian voodoo god provided my wife.

I'm not sure which god was listening to my thanks for the great skiing, view and sky, but the stoned guy under the tree had answered.

After regaining my composure I said, "You're not God are you?"

"No," he said, "I'm just a guy sitting under a tree."

"I knew that," I said wearily. "But you should be careful about who you impersonate. I've never seen a slope this gentle slide, but if you tick-off God, it just might.

Knowing how inaccurate a Heaven-triggered avalanche can be, I got away from that guy. It wasn't until I was almost one thousand feet closer to the highpoint that the missed opportunity dawned on me. Was it possible that I was just in the presence of the Almighty? Could it be that God would be found sitting under a pine tree with a joint in hand? It stands to reason with so many people incorrectly claiming to know God's will that the Creator might be reluctant to appear before some ski-bum-media-hack for fear of being misquoted.

The farther I got from Him the more convinced I was that I might have missed my chance to ask some important questions–questions that have been the subject of debate for decades. Had I the presence of mind, I could have asked Him if there is ever any valid reason for men to wear stretch pants, for anyone to mono-ski or wear those hats with moose antlers on them. It would have been illuminating to find what God's take was on why ski instructors never get cold sores and Kamikaze pilots wore helmets. Yes, there are many out there that think they can answer these and all questions by quoting the Bible. Sorry…I've long given up trusting man's ability to interpret God's will. I'd rather wait to get my orders direct from the horse's mouth. I guess I'll never know.

But on the other hand, whether the guy under the tree was the Creator or just some guy out on snowshoes, he did say something that I'm sure all gods would agree with.

He said, "You're welcome."
You can quote me.

CHAPTER 8: SEX, LOVE, & BODY PARTS

Here is a potpourri of columns many of which I wrote when I was all 'whacked-out' on cold medicine.

SHOPPING FOR DIRTY BOOKS

Various Colorado Newspapers, *June 2003*

Manny went to prison.

The manner of his misdeed isn't important. Suffice to say, he was guilty, he pled as such and is being punished.

When I heard of his situation, I wrote expressing my condolences and offered to send him money, food, books or a hacksaw.

He promptly responded (prisoners make the best pen-pals), thanking me for my consideration.

He wrote that he was well, relatively comfortable and was actually relieved to get his legal hassles over with. He graciously refused my offer for financial help (phew, I was afraid he might call my bluff on that one) and said that the food in prison was not too bad and the library was even better. He then added that if it weren't too much trouble, he would greatly appreciate me sending him any dirty magazines I might have.

I don't buy dirty magazines. I have always maintained that if you have a dirty mind, you don't need dirty literature, but I felt bound by honor to satisfy my good friend's meager request.

I would have no problem going into the local grocery store, where many people know me, to purchase a *Playboy Magazine*. After some of the shopping missions my wife has sent me on, in search of various feminine products, buying a *Playboy* would be a breeze. But

Manny specifically asked me not to send him *Playboy Magazine*.

According to Manny, in the prison culture, *Playboy Magazine* is considered akin to "kissing your sister." He said that in jail, the smut of choice were those "other magazines" featuring misspelled headlines and models with pimples. The ones kept behind the counter.

I live in a small town. It is difficult for me to enter any business without meeting someone I know or someone who knows me. I wasn't looking forward to walking into a convenience store, picking up a Power Bar, a carton of orange juice and a stack of porn.

Human sexuality is as confusing and bizarre as a slumber party at Michael Jackson's house. For animals (and some Catholics), mating is mostly confined to one season a year and then forgotten until the internal calendar once again reads breeding time. Not so for the human species.

We're obsessed with the thought, the idea, the possibility and the inkling of a chance for physical love. We pass foolish laws determining who can marry, what part of the human body is obscene and even what sex act is legal. Our government spends millions to promote teen abstinence while at the same time society encourages teens to dress like Britney Spears.

We have turned love into a spectator sport.

The average person spends much more time doing housework than making love (I wish I'd married an average person), but you don't find many vacuuming magazines on the racks.

I personally feel there is nothing wrong with soft or hardcore porn as long as there is no coercion of the participants and that it doesn't involve children. In countries with more liberal pornography and prostitution laws there seems to be fewer crimes of a sexual nature. It has been argued that those materials and practices provide some essential outlets for would-be offenders.

In a perfect world, those outlets wouldn't be required, but after thousands of years of self-imposed guilt and insecurity the human animal needs to emotionally evolve a little before we can ascend to the sexual maturity of a monkey.

Some would contend that the sexual media degrades women, and I guess that I would have to agree. At the least, it is their choice and they are compensated. Most of us have been degraded for cash—for me, it has been on radio and television.

The bigger question is why some people—not in prison—choose paper and film over flesh and blood.

That said, I was still reluctant to walk boldly into the Seven Eleven and say to the clerk, "My good man, give me a stack of your finest smut."

But I was not about to be dictated to by archaic morals imposed on me by a repressive society. My intentions were good and my motives pure. If I could provide a small amount of pleasure for a person isolated from human compassion and the love of his family, why not?

While driving to the convenience store, I steeled myself for the stares and ridicule that were sure to follow. I filled up my truck with gas, approached the cashier and upon further reflection decided to do my errand next time I worked in Denver...

~~~

NO IF, ANDS OR BUTTS

Various Colorado Newspapers, *September 2002*

"If I said I was the best in the world, I'd be bragging. If I said I wasn't. I'd be lying."

Rocky Marciano, the undefeated Heavyweight Boxing Champion, said that. This was back during a time when athletes were expected to be humble. The statement made headlines; the sportswriters deemed the "Brockton Blockbuster" cocky. A few decades earlier, when the press suggested that Dizzy Dean was "too big for his own britches," he retorted, "It ain't bragging if you can do it."

I feel a little like Dizzy Dean tonight, but I'm simply telling the truth when I say I have a prostate of a man half my age.

Please don't misinterpret this. I don't have a prostate *from* a man half my age—it is not a transplant. Rather, *mine* is in the mint condition of man in his mid-twenties.

I didn't even know what a prostate was until I turned forty. At that time, older friends gleefully told me that I had to get it checked once a year. I asked my sister-in-law, a nurse, to show me one in an anatomy book. My comment: "Man, that seems a hard spot to work on; how do you get to it?" When she told me, I thought she was kidding.

Men are like dogs and customs agents—we can smell fear. It was for that reason I wasn't able to get a straight answer concerning the actual discomfort involved in a prostate exam. Keith said it was rather pleasant; Craig admitted there was some discomfort involved; Sam said it felt like getting a scalp massage, administered from the inside.

For the uninitiated, the prostate is located on the opposite end of the body from your cowlick. It is the size of a plum, and has something to do with sex and reproduction. According to statistics, ninety-percent of men who live to be ninety will get prostate cancer. This does not mean that they will necessarily die from it. It means that after a death from something else, ninety-percent will show the condition when examined. For men over forty, it is the single most likely health issue to cause alarm. It is fairly easy to treat if caught in time, so that is why men my age should be checked at least every couple of years. Without going into gory details, the procedure is much like a tonsil exam, but from the opposite end.

Considerably more painful, yet less embarrassing is the accompanying blood test. The beauty of the blood work, called PSA, is that the lower the number returned from the test result, the better. Anything under four is normal and under two exceptional. Any number below one is a prostate worth bragging about. The quantifiable digit makes for lively competition. Currently there are three of my friends, of similar age, who compete in the "Prostate of the Year" competition. We all are tested within a couple of weeks, meet for beers and reveal the results—the best butt wins. I'm undefeated.

I've tried to not let my prostate go to my head, but at this point in my life there is very little else to brag about. While other men boast of careers, homes and possessions, my prostate is where I'm able to toot my own horn. I must point out that all my bud's butts were also at an exceptional mark, but none could hold a candle to mine.

Obviously, the purpose of this story is not to simply brag of the grandeur of my gland. It is to remind all of you in and around forty to join in on the competition. Both tests are relatively painless and inexpensive. Do yourself a favor, bite the bullet and get it done. Ask for Doctor Randy, tell him I sent you and he'll give you a lollipop...

~~~

A WORKING CLASS LOVE STORY

Various Colorado Newspapers, *December 2004*

Pat and Mike were two regular people, raised during a time when regular people had fewer choices.

Even at the end of his life when Mike had difficulty remembering the names of his six kids, he could retell the story of his first meeting with Pat.

They met at a diner in Brockton, Massachusetts, a town nicknamed "Shoe Factory City U.S.A."

She was thirteen; he was twenty-one.

The depression was winding down and Mike worked in a factory, while Pat was a maid. He was treating himself to a rare restaurant-cooked grilled cheese sandwich and she was picking up lunch for the rich lady for whom she worked.

He was poor, skinny and wearing dirty clothes. His hands stained from leather dye. He approached her, and in his best Errol Flynn voice said, "Hello, Red, where have you been all my life." (She would later admit it was love at first sight, but she did a good job hiding it.)

"It's Miss O'Malley to you. You better get back to your sandwich...you don't look like you can afford to miss a meal."

Undaunted, he pursued. "My name is Mike. There is a seat open next to me at the counter. I'll buy you a cup of coffee and you can have half of my sandwich. I haven't touched it."

How could she refuse such an offer? Nine years later they were married.

I suppose by the standards of the day the newly-weds might have been considered lucky. Mike had steady employment and Pat's situation was considerably better than her immigrant mother's at the same age.

Neither of them received much love while growing up and once married they made up for that lost time. Mike was protective and affectionate. He was well aware of the hardship in his wife's past and was determined that she would suffer no more. Pat's love was laced with admiration and gratitude. Here was a man who took her from a life of servitude and gave her respect and a title. When she called him at work, she'd ask for "my hero" and leave love notes in his lunch box.

They would look back and say those were the best years of their lives. They would dance to the radio, make love when the kids were asleep and share their dreams. Self-employment, a big house and nice furniture were dreams. But in the meantime, they had each other.

Good fortune smiled upon Pat and Mike and brought them six healthy kids, a home with a yard and, after fifteen years of labor and saving, Mike's own company.

"Be careful of what you wish for, you might get it," the cynics warn. When they began to be able to afford the things they wanted, they lost the things they had.

The sign in front bore Mike's name—he couldn't be expected to let his help work unsupervised. He soon was working six days a week, then often again heading in to do paper work after church on Sunday. Pat's role was relegated to mother, wife and hostess, but no longer partner.

Pat wasn't sure what was missing in her life. She loved her children and home but felt lonely and neglected. She longed for the days of poverty and love, and would have traded her new bedroom set for one bite of that grilled cheese sandwich they shared on their first date.

Friends would comment how lucky they were, but Pat didn't feel so lucky. She was cooking and cleaning for eight people and felt lonely when her already fragile nerves deteriorated with stress, loneliness and menopause. Like many housewives of her time, Pat was faced with a sense of purposeless desperation. Mike was too busy to be aware of his mate's depression.

Ten years had come and gone, business was good and Mike could afford top shelf whisky. He wished he could spend more time with his kids, but at least they all had good clothes—something he never had. He sometimes would wonder what was wrong with Pat, but he didn't have a lot of time to spend thinking about it because he had a business to run.

Some people never learn. Some never get the chance, but Mike was lucky. The doctor said the heart attack should have killed him, but didn't.

For four months, Pat nursed him back to health. Work was out of the question, and with the help of his oldest son the business seemed to run itself. They got reacquainted, Mike stopped drinking and gambling and Pat finally shared her feelings. Mike's strength returned as did Pat's confidence. Soon, they were once again dancing to the radio.

Mike never went back to work, the house was paid for and in those days Social Security meant something. He would sometimes grow depressed over the years he had wasted and apologized to his wife, but Pat wouldn't tolerate his melancholy. She would hold him in her arms and say, "Shut up you damn fool. You ain't much, but you're all mine."

Mike died at the age of ninety, a widower. During his last days, delirium set in. (He looked over at his youngest daughter and said, "I have a date with a thirteen year old.") He passed that night.

On paper, Pat and Mike's lives might seem ordinary. But they weren't characters out of a book, they were two people doing the best they could under the circumstances. They were my parents.

~~~

FIRST STEP TAKEN IN THE LIFE OF A TOILET CRIME

Summit Daily News, April 2003

It was like passing through the checkout line at the grocery store with a pack of adult diapers and extra-small condoms. It was a humiliating purchase.

I'm never entirely comfortable at the building center. My hands are too clean, my Carhartts too new and my purchases too small. While the general contractors and tradesmen buy forty-foot ladders and buckets of ten-penny nails, I sheepishly pay for my footstool and curtain rod.

Rather than asking what the difference is between carriage bolts and pan-head screws, I'll buy a dozen of each and see which works.

Our move from a condo into a single-family home made it obvious how lacking I was in manly hardware. It seemed like every cloth hook, towel rack and toilet paper holder requires a different type of screw, molly-bolt or lock-washer. Each discovery of tool and screw deficiencies requires another trip to the store. I've become so intimidated that I started sending my wife in to buy stuff.

After years of being sent to pick up feminine hygiene products, I figured she owed me a push broom or two.

It wasn't until every toilet in the house was clogged that we flipped a coin to see who would go back to the hardware store. I lost and waited for the middle of the day when most of the tradesmen were at their jobsites. I made sure all the items I wanted were marked, so I would not draw attention by requiring a price check. I set my three products on the counter. After ringing up my purchases of a Swisher high-powered bathroom plunger, McDaniel's six-foot toilet auger and a gallon of Let It Flow Pipe Purger, the clerk looked at me and said, "Damn boy, what have you been eating?"

Luckily, I had the presence of mind to blame my wife.

My mate and I thought it was a weird coincidence that as soon as we moved into our new love-shack our digestive juices became tepid.

We never had excessive plumbing problems in our old place. It took only six days living in our new home for us to clog three toilets. After some research and forty-five dollars later, I learned that the problems do not lie in our intestines but rather with the federal government.

About ten years ago, the legislature passed a law that no toilet sold in America can use more than 1.6 gallons of water per flush. Builders and users alike have denounced these so-called low flow toilets.

Yes, they do save water, but they also have the hydraulic flushing power of a baby drooling. There is no denying that they cut the water-per-flush ration of a normal toilet in half.

But this mandates that all who use them switch to a hay-only diet.

I've always known I was a NIMBY (not in my backyard) person. It seems I'm also a NIMB (not in my bathroom) person. I've found if you don't mind breaking the law, there are alternatives.

Just over this country's borders in Canada and Mexico, there are plenty of high flow (5.2 gallons a flush) commodes on the market for the right price.

As I left the Breckenridge Building Center, a toilet bootlegger approached me. He saw me leaving with the three-pack of de-clogging products.

He walked up and whispered, "Hey man, want to buy a toilet?"

"What do you got?" I asked.

"Keep your voice down," he said. "The cops are everywhere. I have a seven-gallon Mexican white porcelain. This baby kicks butt; you could flush a Rottweiler down with one of these things."

We walked to his truck. The back was filled with contraband.

"Where do you get this stuff?" I asked.

"Drove it through customs myself. Pot, coke and speed are deader than fried chicken. The big money is in hot crappers."

The gun freaks like to say that if guns are outlawed only the criminals will have guns. The same thing could be said for toilets. I consider my purchase an act of civil disobedience. I'm breaking an unjust law and willing to pay the consequences. I'll be like Gandhi,

Mandela, Thoreau and Joan of Arc—only different. History will say, "Biff America suffered for his convictions so that others could flush with confidence."

~~~

THE INFAMOUS PRETZEL HOLD

Various Colorado Newspapers, *January 2002*

A good story improves with each telling. Or to put it another way, truth is often overrated. The more an event is recounted; often the more interesting, funny, or poignant that event becomes. This story did not happen to me. My guess is that it is a mix of fact and fiction. I've heard it told a few times, brilliantly. I decided to share the tale, while admittedly adding some personal touches. A warning to my more sensitive readers, this story contains a subject matter that some might consider offensive.

Craig's high school was in the heartland of Iowa with a graduating class of forty-seven. Like many rural schools, two activities were popular with the students: animal husbandry and wrestling, but Craig didn't have the physique for either.

One day, the wrestling coach came into the gym class, took Craig aside and said the wrestling team needed him to lose a match for the team. It wasn't that the coach wanted him to throw the contest—the fact that my friend would lose was a forgone conclusion. There were three wrestlers out with the flu and the team would lose less points if someone competed and lost instead of having to forfeit the match.

As a freshman, Craig had tried out for wrestling, discovered that he wasn't any good and quit. When the coach called upon his school spirit by asking him to lose one for the team, he could not refuse.

There were two reasons that the coach was sure that Craig did not stand a chance. One, he was fighting against the Iowa State Champion, and two, Craig stunk. But that said, a forfeit was twice as costly to the team as a defeat, so my pal suited up. On the bus ride to the competition, the coach briefed his soon-to-be-slaughtered lamb. He told Craig that there was no disgrace in defeat, but there was a possible injury in carelessness.

Craig's opponent had perfected the dreaded "pretzel hold"—a move that the next year would be made illegal in high school competition. The coach told his athlete to not get close enough to his adversary to be caught in the pretzel hold at all cost. He was cautioned that if he was caught, to immediately tap out and quit to avoid injury.

It wasn't until Craig saw his opponent that he began to get scared. Across the mat stood an ape-like farm boy with a pimply face, angry eyes and thick arms that hung nearly to his knees. He didn't respond when my friend smiled. Just before the referee blew the whistle to begin the match, the coach told Craig to "do your best, and lose safely."

The match went as expected, Craig was getting his butt kicked. The good news was that in tribute to his athletic ability and lack of grappling skills, he had thus far avoided the pretzel hold. He got a little cocky and that's when his world turned black.

To hear Craig tell it, one second he was merely getting beaten, the next he was about to pass out. His entire torso was twisted into a human knot. He had no idea which direction was up or down. A searing flash of pain engulfed his body while his eyes closed in agony. He began to yell to the referee to halt the match but could not be heard. He was panicked, frightened and felt he could be seriously injured. Just before losing consciousness, he opened his eyes. In front of his face, he saw the pronounced outline of two testicles covered by the thin fabric of a wrestling uniform. He bit them.

Next thing anyone knew, Craig was back on his feet while his opponent stood by unfazed yet dumbfounded. The match ended soon after with Craig losing hugely on points but with the distinction of being the only opponent to escape the dreaded Pretzel Hold.

When re-telling his story, it is at this point in the narrative that Craig pauses for effect. Generally, the audience waits for an explanation. Eventually someone will ask, "Well, after you...you know, how did you escape?"

My pal will pause again and say, "You'd be surprised at the feats of strength possible when you bite your own testicles."

I just read this story to my buddy John, who wrestled his way through college. He told me that, in his opinion, this story is far-fetched at best, and might be an outright fabrication. But we both agreed, that in some cases, it is better to be entertaining than factual...

ABOUT THE AUTHOR

Boston-born writer, comedian and skier, Jeffrey Bergeron, under the alias Biff America, was the recipient of the 2005 Colorado Press Association award for both humor and serious column writing. Recently elected to the Breckenridge City Council on the homeland security and medicinal marijuana platform, Bergeron skis more days than he works and lives in Breckenridge with his hot wife, Ellen. He can be seen on Resorts Sports Network, heard on KOA radio, and read regularly in Backcountry Magazine and several Colorado newspapers.

More books from Jeffrey Bergeron are available at: http://ReAnimus.com/authors/biff

•

ReAnimus Press

Breathing Life into Great Books

If you enjoyed this book we hope you'll tell others or write a review! We also invite you to subscribe to our newsletter to learn about our new releases and join our affiliate program (where you earn 12% of sales you recommend) at
www.ReAnimus.com.

Here are more ebooks you'll enjoy from ReAnimus Press, available from ReAnimus Press's web site, Amazon.com, bn.com, etc.:

Steep Deep & Dyslexic, by Jeffrey Bergeron

Dear America: Letters Home from Vietnam, by edited by Bernard Edelman for The

New York Vietnam Veterans Memorial Commission

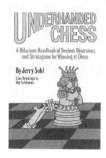

Underhanded Chess, by Jerry Sohl

Underhanded Bridge, by Jerry Sohl

Side Effects, by Harvey Jacobs

American Goliath, by Harvey Jacobs

Beautiful Soup, by Harvey Jacobs

Kafka s Uncle and Other Strange Tales, by Bruce Taylor

Kafka s Uncle: The Unfortunate Sequel,
by Bruce Taylor

Kafka s Uncle: The Ghastly Prequel, by Bruce Taylor

Edward: Dancing on the Edge of Infinity,
by Bruce Taylor

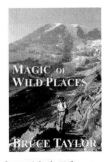

Magic of Wild Places, by Bruce Taylor

Mountains of the Night, by Bruce Taylor

The Gilded Basilisk, by Chet Gottfried

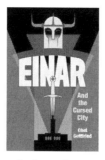

Einar and the Cursed City, by Chet Gottfried

Einar and the Myrtledale Conspiracy, by Chet Gottfried

Into the Horsebutt Nebula, by Chet Gottfried

Innocents Abroad (Fully Illustrated & Enhanced Collectors' Edition), by Mark Twain

The Bleeding Man and Other Science Fiction Stories, by Craig Strete

I've Never Been To Me, by Charlene Oliver

Trilobyte, by Edward Bryant

Wyoming Sun, by Edward Bryant

Cinnabar, by Edward Bryant

Fetish, by Edward Bryant

Neon Twilight, by Edward Bryant

Predators and Other Stories, by Edward Bryant

Darker Passions, by Edward Bryant

Among the Dead and Other Events Leading to the Apocalypse, by Edward Bryant

Particle Theory, by Edward Bryant

The Baku: Tales of the Nuclear Age, by
Edward Bryant

In Hollow Lands, by Sophie Masson

Journals of the Plauge Years, by Norman
Spinrad

Fragments of America, by Norman Spinrad

Pictures at 11, by Norman Spinrad

The Men from the Jungle, by Norman Spinrad

Greenhouse Summer, by Norman Spinrad

Passing Through the Flame, by Norman
Spinrad

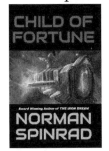

Child of Fortune, by Norman Spinrad

Mexica, by Norman Spinrad

The Mind Game, by Norman Spinrad

The Children of Hamelin, by Norman Spinrad

The Iron Dream, by Norman Spinrad

Bug Jack Barron, by Norman Spinrad

Russian Spring, by Norman Spinrad

Little Heroes, by Norman Spinrad

Past Masters, by Bud Webster

The Starcrossed, by Ben Bova

The Exiles Trilogy, by Ben Bova

The Star Conquerors (Collectors' Edition),
by Ben Bova

Colony, by Ben Bova

The Kinsman Saga, by Ben Bova

The Weathermakers, by Ben Bova

The Multiple Man, by Ben Bova

The Story of Light, by Ben Bova

Immortality, by Ben Bova

Ghosts of Engines Past, by Sean McMullen

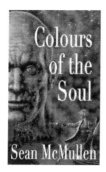

Colours of the Soul, by Sean McMullen

The Cure for Everything, by Severna Park

The Sweet Taste of Regret, by Karen Haber

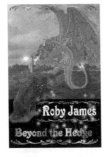

Beyond the Hedge, by Roby James

Commencement, by Roby James

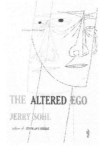

The Altered Ego, by Jerry Sohl

The Odious Ones, by Jerry Sohl

Prelude to Peril, by Jerry Sohl

The Spun Sugar Hole, by Jerry Sohl

The Lemon Eaters, by Jerry Sohl

The Anomaly, by Jerry Sohl

In Search of the Double Helix, by John Gribbin

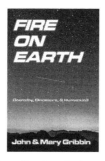

Fire on Earth, by John and Mary Gribbin

Q is for Quantum, by John Gribbin

In Search of the Big Bang, by John Gribbin

Ice Age, by John and Mary Gribbin

FitzRoy, by John and Mary Gribbin

Cosmic Coincidences, by John Gribbin and
Martin Rees

Local Knowledge (A Kieran Lenahan Mystery), by Conor Daly

A Mother's Trial, by Nancy Wright

Bad Karma: A True Story of Obsession and Murder, by Deborah Blum

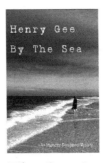

By The Sea, by Henry Gee

The Sigil Trilogy (Omnibus vol.1-3), by
Henry Gee

Made in the USA
San Bernardino, CA
31 March 2019